When Your Son Or Daughter Is Going Through a Divorce

Thomas Whiteman, Ph.D., and Debbie Barr

OLIVER
NELSON

THOMAS NELSON PUBLISHERS
Nashville • Atlanta • London • Vancouver

Published in Nashville, Tennessee, by Thomas Nelson, Inc., Publishers, and distributed in Canada by Word Communications, Ltd., Richmond, British Columbia.

The Bible version used in this publication is THE NEW KING JAMES VERSION. Copyright © 1979, 1980, 1982, Thomas Nelson, Inc., Publishers.

Library of Congress Cataloging-in-Publication Data
Whiteman, Tom.
    When your son or daughter is going through a divorce / Thomas Whiteman and Debbie Barr.
        p. cm.
    Includes bibliographical references (p.).
    ISBN 0-8407-9188-7 (pbk.)
    1. Divorced people—Family relationships.   2. Parent and adult child.
3. Divorce—Psychological aspects.   4. Divorce—Religious aspects—Christianity.
I. Barr, Debbie.   II. Title.
HQ814.W55   1994
306.874—dc20   94-23076
                                                                CIP

Printed in the United States of America.

1 2 3 4 5 6 — 99 98 97 96 95 94

To my mom and dad, Marilyn and Leon Whiteman. They have raised me to love God, trust in Christ, and respect myself and others. Together, we have suffered the pain of divorce in our family. The stability of my parents, their faithful support, and love for me helped me through this very difficult time. Today, they continue to enrich my life and bless my wife, Lori, and me by being wonderful grandparents to our children. Thank you, "Mimi and Pop-Pop."

Tom Whiteman
Paoli, Pennsylvania

To the wonderful friends who stood with me in *loco parentis* (as my parents were no longer living) throughout my separation and divorce.

To my fellow travelers on the bumpy road to divorce: Linda Magers, David Brown, Sheila Mitchell, Mary Bollinger, Mike Minigh, and Andrea Chappell. Your friendship has been a precious gift. I'm so glad we had each other for mutual support and encouragement. It's been an unbelievable journey, but I think we've made it!

To faithful and precious friends Angie Yoran, Beverly Meyst, Lynn and David Hallsey, and Danny and Penny Parrish, with affection and deep gratitude. Thank you for listening patiently, caring, calling, praying, and being there for me. I am also thankful for many other friends (too numerous to list here) who encouraged me and helped me in special ways during my twenty months of separation. I will always be grateful for the way you encircled me during the most difficult time of my life. No one could ask for better friends—y'all are the best!

Finally, to Jackie Camden Mackie, my counselor and my friend. Thank you for parenting me through this crisis. I love you dearly!

Debbie Barr
Winston-Salem, North Carolina

Contents

Preface

This volume was a collaborative effort by Dr. Tom Whiteman and Debbie Barr. As a psychologist and counselor, Tom provided the sound professional expertise which forms the basis for each chapter. In addition, much of the anecdotal material was gleaned from Tom's years of experience counseling many individuals and families in the process of divorce. As a journalist, Debbie's role was to help Tom sculpt the data—personal experience stories, survey responses, and clinical information—into book form. Direct quotes were obtained from personal interviews which Debbie conducted and also from a written survey which was designed together and distributed to the parents of divorcing adult children and to adult children themselves. The names and some details have been modified to protect privacy.

Because this book deals with both men and women, we have used both "he" and "she" interspersed when referring to an adult child or one parent. These pronouns do not imply necessarily that a man is more disposed to react a certain way or that only a woman struggles with certain issues.

Each author has both a personal and a professional interest in the topic of this book. Tom Whiteman is the founder and president of Life Counseling Services in Paoli, Pennsylvania. He is also the president of Fresh Start Seminars, Inc., which conducts divorce recovery seminars throughout the United States. Tom has experienced divorce personally and he draws upon that experience as he speaks to the thousands of divorced persons who attend Fresh Start seminars each year. He has authored or co-authored many divorce recovery materials, including *The Fresh Start Divorce Recovery Workbook*, *The Fresh Start Single Parenting Workbook*, and *Innocent Victims: Helping Children Cope Through the Trauma of Divorce*. Today, Tom is remarried, and he and his wife, Lori, have two daughters, Elizabeth and Michelle, and a son, Kurt.

Debbie Barr holds a B.A. in journalism and is a freelance writer whose work has been published in numerous magazines. She is also the author of *Children of Divorce: Helping Kids When Their Parents Are Apart* and *A Season at Home: The Joy of Sharing Your Child's Critical Years*. Debbie has recently joined the Fresh Start team of divorce recovery speakers. A work-at-home single parent, she is the mother of one son, Christopher.

Introduction

It had been a whirlwind courtship and a fairy tale romance. And now, the long awaited day had come. The organ music floated through the beautifully decorated church, where faithful friends and loving family members had assembled to watch the young man and woman vow their lives to each other for "so long as they both shall live."

Michelle was a radiant, beautiful bride. Robert was a handsome, shy-but-smiling groom. As they swept down the aisle together, arm in arm to start married life together, their parents cried tears of joy. They were so proud of their children. This couple had everything going for them.

No one would ever have guessed that in just a few short years their parents' tears of joy would be turned into tears of deep, unspeakable grief. Michelle and Robert would be divorced.

If you are the parent of an adult child who has experienced, or is presently experiencing, divorce, then you, too, have known the pain that Michelle and Robert's parents felt. You are not alone. With a national divorce rate of 50 percent, most mature parents with two or more children will one day see at least one of their adult children face divorce.

When a son or daughter faces the crisis of divorce, the parents often experience a crisis of their own. They are hit with a flood of emotions: anger, confusion, sorrow, shame, guilt, sadness, and anxiety.

There are more questions than answers: Why did this happen in our family? How can I help my child through this crisis? Did we do anything to contribute to the problem? What will happen to my grandchildren? How should I treat my son-in-law or daughter-in-law? Where is God in this mess?

Many books have been written on the needs of divorcing couples. Many other books are designed to help children through the divorce of their parents. This book, however, is different. It is designed specifically for *you*, a parent whose adult child is going through divorce. This book will address your feelings, fears, and concerns. It will answer many of your questions. It will also help you to be a positive influence in the lives of your children and grandchildren as they experience the difficult days surrounding divorce. And it will give you hope, encouragement, and direction as you and your family develop a new post-divorce lifestyle.

PART I

Understanding and Coping with Your Feelings

1

Why Does It Hurt So Much?

I know God will not give me anything I can't handle. I just wish that He didn't trust me so much.

—Mother Teresa

Divorce. The very word is synonymous with emotional pain. Most of us take for granted the fact that the nuclear family—husband, wife, and any children born of their union—will experience an emotional earthquake when divorce occurs. We realize that extended family members (brothers and sisters, cousins, aunts and uncles) may also be deeply affected. What we may not expect is the degree to which a divorcing couple's parents are uniquely impacted by the breakup.

When adult children divorce, their mature parents may find themselves in the midst of tremendous, possibly unprecedented, emotional pain. *Why does it hurt so much?* The hues of grief can be as varied as the spectrum of family circumstances which surround divorce. Consider these stories.

Bill. When Bill's daughter, Katie, first married, the relationship between Bill and Katie's husband, Jack, was strained. Over time, however, the two men developed a friendship that was nurtured through their common interests. They went sailing together and golfed and fished together as well. The older man grew to think of his son-in-law as a close friend. And the feeling was mutual: Jack regarded Bill with great affection, almost as a second father. But when the marriage between Katie and Jack went sour, the friendship between the two men was thrown into a tailspin. When Jack and Katie divorced, Bill grieved as any father would. But Bill's pain was compounded by the fact that, in the divorce of his daughter, he had lost a dear friend as well.

Katherine. Katherine feels that she is partly to blame for her daughter Jenny's divorce. Years earlier when Jenny had broken off her engagement with her fiancé, Katherine was upset. "He seemed like a wonderful guy," she explains. "I didn't realize how deep-seated his emotional problem was." Jenny and her fiancé got back together and eventually married, but the marriage ended in divorce. Now Katherine feels somewhat responsible. "My daughter knew I was disappointed about the broken engagement. If I had not made my feelings known to her, would she have gone back to him? I did tell her not to marry him to please me." Katherine's grief is twinged with self-blame.

Sarah and Tom. Sarah and Tom adored their three grandchildren and saw them at least once a week. But after their son, Greg, and his wife, Mary Ellen, divorced, Mary Ellen took the kids and moved back to her parents' home, several hundred miles away. Sarah and Tom grieve not only for the broken marriage, but also for their precious grandchildren. They wonder, "Will we ever see them again?"

Mitch. Mitch saw his son, Brent, as a model Christian man. Brent was a good dad and a good husband by every conceivable measure that Mitch could see. When Brent's marriage to Molly broke up, Mitch was shocked. What could possibly have gone wrong? He was devastated to learn that Brent had physically abused Molly.

WHEN THE UNTHINKABLE HAPPENS

Perhaps you can identify with one or more of these parents. Most likely, you are reading this book because you, too, are in pain as a result of the divorce or separation of one of your adult children.

Why does it hurt so much? Few parents expect that their children will become divorce statistics. They love their kids and want them to be happy. Marriage is supposed to be for life. That's why, when divorce comes, it's always a shock. As the authors of *The Grandmother Book* put it, "We start out certain that our families will beat the odds. They will stay together, happily living out their lives, joyfully celebrating special occasions together for years and years and years to come. Then suddenly, at some point, the realities of life confront us and the unthinkable happens."[1] Even if the couple's disharmony is a creeping realization that has dragged on for years, the entire divorce event is still a jolt to our hopes, dreams, expectations, and beliefs. In the face of impending divorce, many parents literally go into shock.

---

1. Jan Stoop & Betty Southard, *The Grandmother Book: Sharing Your Special Joys and Gifts with a New Generation* (Nashville: Thomas Nelson Publishers, 1993), 209.

Jack and Peggy related, "When our son announced plans to divorce his wife, we were so stunned that our response was total silence. We just didn't know how to respond. We didn't know what to say." Peter, whose son's affair preceded his divorce, shared, "Some years earlier we lost a son in an automobile accident. The loss in death was far less traumatic than this son's separation. I would have to say it is the most traumatic thing that ever happened to me."

If your adult child is going through divorce, remember that *you too* are in the midst of a crisis! Don't be too hard on yourself. Instead, treat yourself with as much tenderness and gentleness as you would a good friend who has just undergone major surgery. It will take some time for you and your family to recover from the trauma of divorce.

Many men and women who had experienced divorce were surveyed for this book. One of the things asked was how they thought their parents had been emotionally impacted. These adult children showed sensitivity and compassion and did not fail to recognize the pain their divorce had brought their moms and dads. During the crisis, they may or may not have been emotionally able to express concern for their parents' well-being, but they were certainly aware of their parents' pain. Looking back, they were aware that their parents had felt:

Mike: ". . . hurt, a feeling of betrayal, and helplessness at not being able to do more."

Cynthia: ". . . shock and embarrassment. It was very upsetting for them to find out my husband left me for another woman, and to know that I had to find full-time work."

Cassie: ". . . anger and fear for my future, both financially and emotionally."

SHOCK AND GRIEF

Betty, the mother of a divorced son, said, "I feel I've gone through the grief emotions one would have in a death. But in divorce, everyone must go on living." Betty is right. The pain associated with divorce is very similar to the pain associated with death. The reason, of course, is that divorce actually *is* a death: the death of a marriage. Grief is a normal, natural, and necessary response to the divorce of an adult child.

Elisabeth Kübler-Ross first popularized the stages of grief in her landmark book, *On Death and Dying*. She highlighted five emotional levels people pass through as they deal with the death of a loved one: denial, anger, bargaining, depression, and finally acceptance. It is now well known that these same five stages of grief accompany any personal crisis, whether it be the prospect of major surgery, the loss of a job, or divorce.

THE SLIPPERY SLOPE

The stages of grief, while predictable, do not follow one after the other in an orderly, linear fashion. Instead, the stages mix and mingle with one another. A grieving person can bounce from one stage to another in rapid succession and then repeat the cycle. It's even possible to experience all five stages in the same day. There are no neat, tidy transitions. Instead, grief is more like riding on an emotional roller coaster—way

up, then way down, then around the track again. Fresh Start
has termed this volatile process the *slippery slope*.

The *slippery slope* idea came from an experience author Bob
Burns had as a cadet at Virginia Military Institute. He relates
the incident in his book, *Recovery From Divorce*.

> Two groups of us were marched to a deep pit that had been
> thoroughly soaked with water. It had turned into a slimy,
> slippery mudhole. Four men were picked from each group
> and told to jump into the pit. The goal was simple: The
> men from one group were to get out of the pit as fast as pos-
> sible while keeping the men from the other group in the pit.
>   You can imagine the result of this experience! As soon
> as one man seemed to make it to the top, a hand would
> reach out and grab his ankle. Suddenly he would be
> dragged, feet first, down to the bottom of the hole! Again
> and again, men who thought they would make it to the top
> found themselves mired in the muck of the pit.[2]

People going through the stages of grief are like those men
in that mudhole. Just when you think you are over the worst of
it—bam! A phone call, a holiday, a TV movie reaches out to
grab you by the emotions and pull you back into the pit. As
you read more about the stages of grief in the next three chapters, keep one thing in mind: the stages may seem clear-cut and
neatly organized on paper, but in reality, grief is a "muddy" experience! The intensity and the depth of your emotions may
surprise you, as will the slipperiness of the slope of grief.

---

2. Bob Burns, *Recovery From Divorce: How to Become Whole Again After the Devastation
of Divorce* (Nashville: Thomas Nelson Publishers, 1992), 64–65.

THE SLIPPERY SLOPE

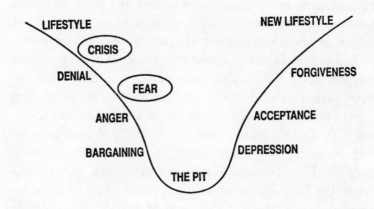

Grief must run its course. There is no such thing as quick grief. For most people, it takes at least two years to grieve the losses of divorce. No matter how badly you may want to skip ahead in the recovery process, grief cannot be hurried. To heal completely, a grieving person must allow time to walk through each stage as it comes, and to be honest about his or her feelings. Take a close look at the chart above. Where are you right now? There is no wrong place to be. Understanding where you are in the process now may give you some idea of what lies ahead.

A GOOD UNDERSTANDING IS HELPFUL

It is reassuring to realize that grief is an entirely normal, inevitable response to divorce. Knowing this assures us that we normal people reacting in a normal way to intense loss and emotional pain. Understanding as much as possible about grief is extremely helpful. The more we know, the more we can be confident that we are processing our pain in a normal fashion, that we are not alone, and that our pain will not last forever.

Unfortunately, the pain and aftershocks of divorce will not disappear in a few days. One reason divorce requires a long recovery period is that divorce is not just one loss but an ongoing series of many losses. We do not realize all of the losses associated with divorce at one time. They unfold as time goes on, often triggering fresh grief. During the first year after divorce, every holiday is laden with potential grief—the first Thanksgiving, the first Christmas, the anniversary date of the now-divorced couple. Many of the losses of divorce are intangible: dashed hopes and dreams, grandchildren who will never be born. These kinds of losses can also contribute to and compound the grief of divorce.

Because the losses of divorce are significant, it will take some time for your family system to regain a sense of emotional equilibrium. That doesn't mean all of you will be in constant misery. Nor does it mean that one day all family members will be completely free from all sorrow and pain concerning the divorce. In reality, especially when there are grandchildren, the implications of a marital breakup persist through the years. But—and this is the good news—after a period of grief and emotional recovery, by taking positive, constructive steps, those touched by divorce can become stronger than they were before.

LOOKING AHEAD

Just now, you may be saddened by the thought that because of divorce, your family will never be the same again. True enough, after divorce, your family will be different than it was before. But you are still a family! Healing takes time. Every divorce also contains the seeds for growth. Families can be stronger, more loving, more caring, and even more closely knit in the wake of divorce. Much depends upon the choices made by the parents and the grandparents. Much depends on you! Even in the midst of your own grief, you can make choices that can either help or hinder your own recovery and the recovery of your family members.

2

Denial and Anger: The Beginning of Grief

Why? Why? Why? Give me a good reason I can hold onto and understand.
—Marie, mother of divorced son

M *om and Dad, I have some bad news. We're getting a divorce.* If you are reading this book, chances are excellent that you have already heard words to this effect from your son or daughter. How did you feel when the meaning of those words sank in? How did you respond emotionally when you realized that your child's marriage was breaking up? Some parents have described what that moment was like for them.

George said, "At first, you hope it's a dream or a nightmare or something." Carol felt "disbelief and terrible sadness." Peggy remembers, "I just felt like the bottom fell out." Alice felt "devastation, fear, disappointment, and frustration." Steven recalls, "I was numbed and shocked. I think it was just utter disbelief." The words Hannah used were "shock, upset, fright, and worry."

For these parents, the news of their child's impending divorce was a total surprise. They never suspected it was coming. The news caught them off guard and jolted them with devastating force. Many of them were dumbfounded or completely mystified, as was Wanda, who says she still has "no idea" why her daughter's marriage broke up. "I thought things were OK," she said. "But evidently, they weren't."

Each of these parents responded to the same kind of awful news in similar ways. None of them could believe what they were hearing. Indeed, none of them wanted to believe what they were hearing! Each of these parents experienced shock, hurt, and disbelief upon learning that their child was about to be divorced.

Other parents, however, were not so surprised. John shared this story.

My son made a very unwise choice when he married his wife. She's a total flirt. She is the kind who knows what it takes to get a man quickly, and she enticed him. It wasn't too long before she was pregnant with his child. They married, even though the families, including myself, showed them all the reasons they ought to choose a different direction. We knew from the beginning that this thing would die unless there was a radical change.

Four years and three affairs later, John's son finally divorced his wife. Says John, "We didn't discover that this divorce was coming—we knew it was coming!"

DENIAL

Whether the news that a child is getting divorced comes as a surprise or whether it is somewhat anticipated, such news always thrusts parents unwittingly onto the slippery slope of grief. *Parents universally respond with some degree of denial.* Denial is a normal reaction to circumstances that are beyond our control. Denial occurs when we don't want to face a painful

fact or circumstance even though we know it is true. Denial
serves as a "shock absorber" that enables a person to maintain
relative normalcy in the midst of abnormal pressures. A person
in denial attempts to avoid a harsh reality and acts as if it does
not exist. He wants to isolate himself from the pain of truth.
The classic phrase of denial is "I can't believe this is happening
to me!" Denial nourishes the secret hope that all of this is, as
George said previously, "a dream or a nightmare or something."

In the short term, denial is not a bad thing. Denial is a
God-given emotional defense mechanism that helps us get
through the first difficult days or weeks of a crisis. It is a natural, normal method of handling shock initially. It protects us
from experiencing too much pain; it prevents an emotional
overload. During an emotional crisis, one's emotional system
responds in the same way. Denial serves a useful purpose, and it
is good to be in denial while everything within you is scream-
ing, "No! This should not be taking place!"

Coping with the Pain

In her book *Mourning Song*, Joyce Landorf compares denial
to a special oxygen mask for use when the whirlwind of a crisis
has sucked every ounce of air out of us. We breathe in the
breath of denial, and it helps us to deal with the intense pain of
the moment. However, if denial is used as an ongoing method
of coping, it can produce destructive results. People who dwell
in denial can become superficial and dishonest. They often
look for the easy way out instead of coming to terms with the
truth. Prolonged use of denial can actually hinder a person's
ability to handle real life.

In his book *Growing Through Divorce*, Jim Smoke tells of

speaking to a group on this subject when suddenly a wedding ring flew past his nose. It hit the wall behind him and rolled back to his feet. He bent down and picked up the ring. "Does this belong to someone in here?" he asked. From the back of the room came the reply: "It did belong to me. But I have been divorced now for over six years. I guess it's about time that I took it off."

That's unhealthy denial—putting up a long-term facade for your friends, your acquaintances, and yourself. It is creating a fantasy world where things are so much better than the way they are in real life.

Marcy's frustration was that her mother-in-law "did not want to believe that her son did anything wrong. My husband became a habitual adulterer. The affairs began after nine and a half years of marriage. The last two years of our marriage, my husband was having affairs with two women at the same time." Marcy's mother-in-law would not emerge from her fantasy of how things "should be" long enough to see things as they really were.

Denial must be considered a short-term coping method. Choosing to live in a perpetual state of numbness is a problem worse than the divorce that is taking place. Problems are never solved and growth never occurs by shutting one's eyes. Mark 8:31–32 provides an example of denial in the life of Peter. Jesus had just spoken of His coming death. He explained that He must suffer many things and be rejected by the elders, chief priests, and teachers of the Law. He told His disciples that He must be killed and after three days rise again. This was too much for Peter! None of this scenario fit into his preconceived understanding of Jesus' purpose. He refused to believe the Lord and even rebuked Him for speaking that way. Peter was experiencing denial to the point where he would not even listen to the truth.

Facing the Facts

Change is never comfortable. The greater the change, the higher the level of discomfort. Discomfort is caused by fear of the unknown: What's going to happen as a result of this change? Will my daughter have to go back to work? Will my grandchildren be all right? Will people at church think we were bad parents? Fear keeps us paralyzed in denial when it is time to be moving on in the healing process. Often we want to protect our image as "good parents" or "good Christians." So, we try to keep the situation quiet. We wait for God to perform a miracle to restore the child's marriage and save us from embarrassment.

Denial can never change reality. But to move past this stage, we must face our fears and resign ourselves to the emotional discomfort. Sooner or later we must admit to ourselves, our friends, our church, and our extended family, that our children are getting a divorce.

This is best accomplished by a gentle, yet firm confrontation with the truth: Will my son or daughter reconcile with his or her mate? Will my family be restored to wholeness? Maybe. Then again, maybe not. But for the time being face circumstances as they are right now—today. It is never a lack of faith to accept reality. On the contrary, it is a *sign* of faith—who but God can provide sufficient wisdom and strength to face the present moment?

ANGER

When we turn our backs on denial to embrace reality, the "Oh, no—not in our family!" of denial turns to "Oh, *yes*—in *our* family." At this point, all of the emotions held back by denial suddenly come rushing in, and parents invariably become angry. They may be angry at themselves, their child, their daughter- or son-in-law, the "other woman" or "other man," the legal system—or God.

This is the next stage of grief. Anger is a relationship response. It is the opposite of indifference. We generally feel anger toward people who are important to us. The fact that we feel any anger toward someone indicates a high level of involvement with that person. This explains why the anger that divorce engenders can be so intense, hostile, and enduring. There are a lot of "villains" in every divorce situation, so there are plenty of places to direct anger.

Resentment

Many parents are simply angry that, at this stage in life, they should have to be going through this kind of agony. Most mature parents expect that the years they spent raising their children and working hard to provide for them should entitle them to the right to relax, to travel, and to tend to their own interests and concerns once those children are grown and married. When an adult child divorces, parents often find that the retirement years include stresses and problems they never planned on. A depressed daughter may move back home. A discouraged son may need financial help. Sometimes grandparents must roll up their sleeves and become parents again, taking on the challenge of raising grandchildren during their retirement years.

Parents who were themselves divorced and struggled to raise their children as single parents or in a "blended" family, may have vowed that this would never happen to their kids. They may be frustrated beyond words to find history repeating itself.

Two of Peggy's four children are divorced. The accumulation of years of heartache, problems, and stress weighs heavily on her. She says, "I guess I always thought when my children grew up and got married I wouldn't have that care burden that I have always had for them. And I thought once they got married everything would be rosy. But that's not true. I feel as responsible for them now as I did when they were little."

Guilt

Parents often become self-critical when their child faces divorce. Carol says that her initial reaction to the divorce was, "What did *we* do wrong?" Anne and her husband reacted similarly. She explains, "It made us, I guess, embarrassed. Sort of like it may have been something we did or something we could have prevented. It was an embarrassing situation."

The pain of guilt and embarrassment may prompt parents to grill themselves mercilessly with hard questions: Did we do something that contributed to their problems? Should we have done more? Called more, had them over to dinner more often? Should we have done less—were we too intrusive? Didn't we raise our child right? Weren't we good role models?

Guilt is really anger turned inward. Parents who feel guilty are angry at themselves.

Understanding Anger

Most people tend to think of anger in negative terms. Many of us grew up in families where we were taught that it was always wrong to be angry. We may have seen anger improperly handled and observed the pain and confusion it caused. Anger may have been expressed actively in sarcasm, criticism, impatience, or physical violence, or passively in stubbornness, self-pity, or withdrawal. Either way, experience has taught that anger is destructive. No wonder so many of us think of anger as something to be avoided at all costs.

The truth is that anger in and of itself is not wrong. Anger is simply a feeling, an emotion. Emotions are neither right nor wrong. *The way that we handle our emotions* is either right or wrong. Feelings of anger and the expression of anger are two different things. Ephesians 4:26 says, "Be angry, and do not sin."

Everyone has feelings of anger. They are God-given. Even Jesus experienced anger—significant anger—toward the Pharisees and the money changers in the temple (see Matt. 23:27; Mark 11:15–17). Our capacity to feel anger affirms that we are created in the image of God: Injustice, cruelty, abuse, neglect, immorality, and many other things stir our hearts to anger, just as they stir the heart of God.

Anger Management

God, of course, always handles His anger in entirely appropriate, responsible ways. Our challenge is to learn how to do the same. We are personally accountable for the ways that we speak and act in response to our feelings of anger. Anger creates an enormous amount of energy—energy that demands expression. We always have four options available to us when we become full of anger. Two of these options are negative, and therefore undesirable, and two are positive.

Rage

Rage, which is sometimes called *catharsis*, is the venting of anger. When rage is vented on other people, the results can be devastating, whether the target is the perceived enemy or an innocent victim. Venting rage on objects is not much better, even though it at least assures that no one will be hurt. Instead of diffusing rage, venting it often increases and compounds anger to the point where a person may lose control. In other words, venting rage solves nothing; it may even enlarge the problem.

Proverbs 29:11 says that "a fool vents all his feelings." Clearly, rage is not a healthy form of anger management.

Repression

The second negative way to handle anger is repression. Repression means that a person just quietly swallows the anger, holding all of anger's volcanic energy inside the body.

The problem with repression is that sooner or later the energy of anger must manifest itself in some way. Often this is in the form of physical or emotional problems: heart attacks, paralysis, strokes, and ulcers. The body may also have weakened defenses against the effects of stress and fatigue, resulting in lesser illnesses such as colds or flu. Serious emotional problems such as depression, excessive fault finding, irritability, or hyperactivity can also stem from repression of anger.

Repression is a popular way to deal with anger because our culture says that outbursts of rage are inappropriate but it's perfectly acceptable to have something wrong with our physical bodies.

Positive Ways to Handle Anger

Ultimately, the most positive way to deal with anger is to go to the person with whom you are angry and resolve the problem. But let's face it—few people are ready to do that until they have worked through a considerable amount of grief. That takes time. Until you reach the point of acceptance and forgiveness, the best approach is redirection.

Redirection

Redirection takes the energy of anger and channels it in a positive direction. Redirection must be a conscious decision: to take the energy-laden feelings and invest them in a positive way. Here are some examples.

In Mark 3 we read how Jesus redirected his anger. The Bible says that He had gone into a synagogue where there was a man with a withered hand. The religious leaders were watching Him to see if they could come up with some accusation against Him (remember, they hated Him and wanted Him dead). Verse 5 says, "And when He had looked around at them with anger, being grieved by the hardness of their hearts, He said to the man, 'Stretch out your hand.' And he stretched it out, and his hand was restored as whole as the other." Jesus took His natural feelings of anger and channeled them into a constructive action that produced a positive result in the life of a hurting man.

Another example of redirected anger is M.A.D.D. (Mothers Against Drunk Drivers). This is an organization founded by mothers whose children have been killed by intoxicated drivers. Instead of taking a .357 Magnum and blowing away the guilty drivers, these moms rechanneled their angry energy into working for public awareness and getting laws changed.

How about you? What is the best way to redirect your angry energy? You may be able to use some of it to help your family. Perhaps your daughter's home is in need of repair and you are handy with hammer and nails. Maybe your grandson needs help learning how to play tennis.

But maybe you are geographically distant, or circumstances are such that you really can't do much to help in your immediate family. Instead of worrying, pacing the floor, or making angry phone calls, choose to redirect your anger into something positive in your own life.

In many cases, it's best to start small. For example, tackle some household projects that require physical energy—painting the spare bedroom, weeding the garden, refinishing furniture. If you are in good health, and your doctor consents, join a league or sign up for lessons to participate in physical activities you especially enjoy, like golf, tennis, swimming, or bowling. If you are employed, expend that extra energy to become a better employee.

We also need to feel as if we are making a difference in the lives of others. Determine to use some excess energy for an excellent cause. Your church office, choir, or nursery; the Red Cross; Habitat for Humanity; the local crisis pregnancy center; Big Brothers or Big Sisters; hospitals; adult literacy groups; the Gideons; soup kitchens—organizations like these are always looking for volunteers. If you know other parents whose adult children are in the process of divorce right now, you may take on the task of organizing a support group!

Resolution

The second positive way to handle anger is resolution. Resolution means openly acknowledging that you are angry but committing to working through your feelings honestly with the person (or persons) who has angered you.

You may be thinking, "I can't do that! I can't even talk to this person!" Lest you find yourself on a false guilt trip, remember that timing is crucial. Resolution is rarely possible during the early stages of a divorce. Right now, there may be too much tension, too many loose ends, too many painful feelings. But in time, resolution is possible, at least from your end of the situation. Most often resolution is best accomplished in the final phase of the grief process, which is the acceptance stage. You can set resolution as an ultimate goal. Eventually, you want to be able to run into your ex-daughter- or son-in-law in the grocery store and be able to converse without feeling awkward.

Resolution recognizes that anger is usually a relational problem between persons. Therefore, when a person desires to resolve his anger, he takes this relational dynamic seriously. The principle of resolution is based on two passages in Matthew.

Matthew 5:23–24: "Therefore if you bring your gift to the altar, and there remember that your brother has something against you, leave your gift there before the altar, and go your way. First be reconciled to your brother, and then come and offer your gift."

Matthew 18:15: "Moreover if your brother sins against you, go and tell him his fault between you and him alone. If he hears you, you have gained your brother."

How interesting: Whether someone has something against you (see Matt. 5), or whether you have something against another person (see Matt. 18), the responsibility to seek reconciliation is always yours! We are to take the initiative in restoring relationships.

Do keep in mind, however, that with a divorce, restoration is often years down the road. Peggy is an example of someone on the way to forgiveness, but honest enough to admit that she is not there yet. Peggy's anger has been directed primarily at her son's new wife—the "other woman." It has been three years since this person entered the picture, but Peggy still says, "I don't want to be around her. I don't want anything to do with her." She admits, "I can't forgive her." When asked how she might feel in five years, she replies, "I hope I will have gotten to that forgiving spirit, because as a Christian, I should. But right now, I can't."

With God's help, eventually Peggy can become an agent of healing and forgiveness within her family. She will know when the time is right! The same is true for you. Even when you sense that you are ready to begin the restoration process, you may find that the other party is not willing. You need not feel guilty or blocked by that person's response or attitude. You are only responsible for your part. When you have said and done what you believe you need to do, you can release both the person and the relationship into the care of God.

3

Bargaining and Depression:
The Midst of Grief

One of the toughest things in the world is when everyone is trying to be bright and cheery and you hurt so bad you feel like you're going to suffocate. It's like salt on an open wound. Yes, I had some tough times of depression.
—Peter, father of divorced son

Bargaining and depression are the intermediate phases of the grief cycle. People tend to spend more time in these two stages than in any of the earlier or later stages of grief.

BARGAINING

When a son or daughter's marriage looks as though it is headed for divorce, parents naturally want to do whatever they can to fix the problem. Bargaining can be defined as the attempt to find quick, simple solutions to complex problems. You might think of it like taking a Crock-Pot recipe and trying to zap it to completion in the microwave. Even a novice cook knows it just won't work!

Similarly, there are no "microwave solutions" to something as complicated as divorce. Yet because we are human, we want everything to be fixed *right now*. We already have discovered that denial doesn't help, and that anger makes things worse. So

25

we emerge from our anger ready to bargain: We'll do anything to make the pain go away and make our family "nice" again.

Ways Parents Bargain

Bargaining usually reflects the priorities or major concerns of a person. It really amounts to an attempt to control or manipulate the situation in the direction we want it to go. The following are some of the ways in which parents bargain when their child's marriage is coming apart.

Bargain #1: They May Apply Pressure for Reconciliation

Wendy's parents told her, "We can't accept this. You can't do this. This isn't right. If you try one more reconciliation attempt, then we'll accept it. But if you don't try it one more time, we'll always feel that you didn't do what you should have." Wendy and her husband had already tried reconciling their relationship three times, but to no avail. Wendy's heart wasn't in it, but solely to please her parents, she agreed to try again. Wendy took her husband back, but, as before, he refused to give up his relationship with his girlfriend. When they had a big fight and her husband stormed off in a huff, Wendy called her parents to say, "See? It didn't work." At that point, Mom and Dad finally were satisfied that Wendy had done all she could. (Wendy had known it all along.)

Bargain #2: They Orchestrate Get-Togethers

Bob and his wife, Bonnie, had been separated for several months. When Bob accepted an invitation to a family Christmas party at his parents' home, he never dreamed that Bonnie would be there, too. Bonnie had appreciated the invitation and had accepted, assuming that Bob would not be there. The evening turned out to be terribly awkward for the separated couple, certainly nothing like the fairy-tale reconciliation Bob's parents may have imagined. Bob left early, and Bonnie ended up in the kitchen crying to her sister-in-law.

Bargain #3: They Try to Set Their Son or Daughter Up with Dates

Many mature parents grew up believing that a person is not "complete" without a mate, and that a single person is not a whole person. As soon as the ink dries on the divorce decree, they are busy playing matchmaker for their adult child.

Bargain #4: They Rescue

The bargaining strategy that some parents use is "just leave everything to me." They believe that the best quick fix is to take care of everything for their son or daughter. If they are convinced that it is best for their daughter to get away from her rotten spouse, they do whatever it takes to make it happen. They move their daughter out of her home, set her up in a new apartment, furnish the place, and agree to pay all the bills.

Parents who rescue still feel responsible for their adult children. They view their child's decisions and problems as *their* decisions and problems. As a result, they take on responsibilities that really belong to the adult child. These parents fail to see that rescuing their child from a bad marriage, financial problems, or emotional pain will only hamstring the child. Rescuing an adult child deprives him of the opportunity to learn from his mistakes. Mothers and fathers who rush in to pay the fine, make the excuses, or mediate the dispute only guarantee that their child will never learn to be responsible for her own actions.

"But, wait a minute!" you may be thinking. "Shouldn't I help my son or daughter at all?" The key is seeing the difference between rescuing and helping. This has to do with a proper understanding of *boundaries:* Whose problems are these? Whose responsibilities are these? When children become adults, parents are no longer responsible *for* them; they are responsible *to* them. There is an important difference! Chapter 7 discusses these issues in more detail.

Bargain #5: They Run Away

The easiest solution is simply to say, "It's not my problem. I don't want to hear about it." If rescuing is at one end of the scale of involvement, running away is at the other. Running away puts distance between parent and child. But like rescuing, running away helps no one. Parents who run abdicate their proper role in their adult children's lives at a time when family members need each other's support and encouragement. Again, Chapter 7 deals with this issue in more detail.

The Real Issue: Control

When parents engage in bargaining tactics, it is because they believe they have some power to effect a change in the situation. But bargaining is a frustrating undertaking! *The real issue is control.* Standing on the sidelines of a divorce-in-progress is difficult: At least if it were your own divorce you would have a legitimate right to try to control the outcome. But this is not your divorce; it is your child's divorce. And parents have no real power to change the situation. This is the hard lesson many parents learn through failed attempts at bargaining.

There is no need to feel guilty about wanting to bargain. The desire to bargain is like running a fever when you have the flu. It is a symptom of the crisis. It indicates that we are normal people in the midst of grief. We should no more feel guilty for attempting to bargain than we would feel guilty for running a fever. It's very natural to want to solve or escape pain and problems. But just as a fever eventually runs its course, so does the bargaining phase of grief.

When bargaining fails and parents rightly conclude that they are not in control, they soon begin to feel hopeless—that the situation is beyond repair. Almost every parent surveyed for this book indicated that he or she felt *powerless*. Most indicated that feeling powerless was their most overwhelming struggle. This point of powerlessness and despair is the next phase of grief: depression.

THE BLACK HOLE OF DEPRESSION

Depression has been defined in many ways. Some say it is like being in a black hole. Others say it is the feeling of being immobilized. Perhaps a Ziggy cartoon expresses it as well as anything else. The sun is shining all around, but Ziggy has his own personal rain cloud pouring down on him wherever he goes. That is depression!

Depression is a normal reaction to the divorce of one's child. It is a normal part of grief. This is *reactive depression*, a low-grade depression that results from an ongoing feeling of powerlessness: "This divorce is going to take place and there is nothing I can do about it. My family will never be the same again."

There are many other discouragements and losses that parents must cope with in the aftermath of divorce. Many grandparents are saddened to discover that they have limited contact with their grandchildren after divorce. They may be discouraged about the way divorce impacts their family traditions and holidays from this point forward. Many struggle with feelings of guilt or social embarrassment. If parents belong to churches that condemn rather than support the divorced, they may feel unsure about how to treat their child and their son-in-law or daughter-in-law. All of these things are, in a word, *depressing*.

Depression is commonly characterized by several things. These are: *Sadness*. You feel low in spirit, hopeless, and helpless. There seems to be a sense of darkness in your life. *Pessimism*. The negative consequences of divorce seem to carry over to all the other areas of life. *Decreased interest in health and personal appearance*. Exercise, diet, rest, and personal grooming may suffer as a result of sadness and pessimism. *Withdrawal*. You may not feel like participating in hobbies, organizations, and other activities that brought pleasure in the past. You may not feel like being with friends, either.

Not surprisingly, many parents stay depressed for a long time, particularly when the divorce or the settlement is dragged on for an extended period of time. George and Anne, who were quoted earlier, both became depressed and struggled to overcome it. George says, "I finally got over it, but it was very, very difficult." Anne recalls, "I was depressed also, over a lot of things: because my husband was not well, because things were not going well—it was a series of depressions."

What's Good About Depression

Take another look at the slippery slope chart in chapter one. Note the location of depression: Depression is the pit. The good news is that once you hit the pit of depression, there is nowhere to go but up! You have to hit bottom before you can turn things around. Depression feels bad, but it signifies that some good things are happening. Here's what's good about depression.

1. When We Reach the Pit of Depression, We Have Gone Through All the Other Stages and Realized That They Don't Work

Counselors know that when people come to the point of depression, it's because they have realized that they are not in control and that they really do need to give up. Denial didn't make the problem go away. Anger did not solve anything and may even have made things worse. Bargaining was frustrating because the people involved didn't do what the person wanted them to do. At the end of all that, there is only depression: "I give up." But this is actually a very good place to be.

2. Depression Means That We Are Beginning to Look at the Problem Honestly

Arriving at depression means that, now, for the first time, you are dealing with the problem in an honest, realistic way. Admitting you are not in control is reality. Denying the problem was not dealing with the situation realistically. Trying to escape the pain was not dealing with the circumstances realistically. Trying to manipulate people was not realistic either. But when we get to the point of facing the pain, we are finally dealing in reality.

3. Depression Makes Us Take a Look Inside Ourselves

Up to this point, the focus has been on everyone else. ("If only she hadn't . . ." "If God would just answer my prayer. . ." "Why didn't he . . . ?") Depression is the first stage where the spotlight turns inward.

The self-examination that takes place during depression can be very beneficial so long as it does not turn into self-condemnation. Even though the divorce is not your divorce, and the problems are not yours to solve, this can be a time to take a look at yourself. *What can I learn about myself from this situation? About our family? How can I be a better parent? A better grandparent? What do I need to do differently in these relationships from now on?*

4. Depression Motivates Us to Look for Help Outside Ourselves

So long as we are in denial, we do not deal with the problem. So long as we are angry, we point the finger at other people. So long as we are bargaining, we try to solve the problem ourselves. But when we reach the stage of depression, we are usually ready to seek help.

Help can come from many places. Many parents seek pastoral counseling or professional therapy for themselves as well as recommending it to their child at this time. In addition, there are other areas where most parents can find valuable support.

Friends—Peter and Marie, whose son had been very active in their church, enlisted twenty-five people at church to spend an hour a week praying for their son. Jack and Peggy found that sharing with friends was helpful to their friends as well as to themselves. Jack said, "I found out that by sharing our hurts it helped some other people who were going through some of the same things—they were going through divorces themselves."

One word of caution: Not all of your friends may understand your pain, and not everyone is equipped to listen and sympathize in the way that you need just now. Find a few friends who are willing to invest the time and energy to listen and perhaps to pray with you. Parents who have "been there" may be most likely to understand.

God—You may be wondering, "If I'm a Christian, isn't it wrong to be depressed? I mean, what about joy and all of that?" You can be sure that God understands how you feel. Remember, He created your emotional response system; He knows all about the grief cycle! God designed our bodies to handle only so much stress and conflict. When we absorb as much as we can take, depression acts like a circuit breaker in an electrical system. When a dangerous electrical overload hits, a circuit breaker clicks off the power to protect the system. Similarly, God designed us so that when we face an emotional overload, the breaker of depression clicks off to give time to restore emotional energy and to help us cope.

The God who knows you intimately is a God of compassion and tenderness. Second Corinthians 7:6 says that God "comforts the downcast." The Psalms provide a wellspring of readings to comfort a depressed and hurting heart. God knows right where you are emotionally and exactly what you need. You can cast "all your care upon Him, for He cares for you" (First Peter 5:7).

Books and Other Resources—Sometimes the best counselor is a good book or an audio tape. Certainly the price is right (compared to the cost of professional therapy), and we can absorb the information comfortably at our own pace. Some of the parents who have shared their stories cited books that were meaningful in their healing process. Joan was encouraged by the book *Parents in Pain*. Marie was so helped by a book called *Good Grief* that she and her husband have purchased hundreds of them over the years and given them away to others who were hurting.

A Final Word About Depression

Reactive depression is, as the name implies, a reaction to an event. This kind of depression is not clinical. It is like a "time out" that gives us pause for reflection and rest. But when depression gives rise to thoughts about life not being worth living, a person may be experiencing a clinical depression which may require professional help. If you think that you, your spouse, your children, or even your grandchildren are experiencing more than reactive depression, seek out professional help as soon as possible. This is especially important if there is a family history of depression or if the depression has persisted for more than three or four weeks. If you don't know where to turn, call your family doctor or a trusted pastor who can direct you to a good counseling resource in your community.

MOVING ON TOWARD THE END OF GRIEF

Depression often creates within us a new humility as we realize that we do not have all the answers. This humility can stimulate greater openness to what we are seeing of ourselves and launch us on a quest for truth. In this way, depression, while painful, can also become one of our greatest teachers. The fact that you have reached depression means that you are closer to acceptance—and closer to the end of the grief experience.

4

Acceptance and Forgiveness: The End of Grief

You know, by this happening to us I am able to sympathize with others who are going through this. It has made me more caring.
—Peggy, mother of two divorced children

The stages of acceptance and forgiveness signal the beginning of the end of the grief process. How quickly parents arrive at this phase has much to do with how well their children and grandchildren are progressing. That is, as they make progress, you make progress, too.

Typically, it takes two years or longer for divorce-related grief to run its course. Every divorce and every family is unique; there are many variables which can affect the timetable. How traumatic the changes are, how cooperative the family members are, and how closely involved the relationships—all will affect the length of the grief period.

ACCEPTANCE—EASIER SAID THAN DONE

Acceptance can be defined in various ways. One definition is "coming to terms with a problem and then continuing to grow, refusing to be preoccupied with the past." Another definition can be found in the words of the apostle Paul in Philippians 4:11: "I have learned in whatever state I am, to be content." Reinhold Niebuhr's famous Serenity Prayer gives insight to the attitude of acceptance:

> God, give us grace to accept with serenity the things that cannot be changed, courage to change the things which should be changed, and the wisdom to distinguish the one from the other.

Acceptance doesn't just happen. You don't wake up one morning and suddenly find yourself in the acceptance stage. Like the other stages of grief, it is a phase you grow into over a period of time.

Accepting the divorce of an adult child, with all of the implications for the family, is much easier said than done. Most people claim to be in the acceptance stage long before they actually are. Many parents think they've arrived, but a single incident or unexpected conversation can throw them all the way back down the slippery slope once again.

Acceptance becomes easier for parents who see that their children and grandchildren seem to be coping reasonably well. When the grandchildren's grades improve after a period of academic difficulty or your daughter finally finds a good job, you feel better. Each new adjustment in their lives relieves the load of concern.

Over time, parents may even begin to see some positive effects of divorce. Until they see these with their own eyes, most parents don't believe there *are* any positive effects! Such was the case with Harry.

When Harry was in the bargaining stage of his grief over

his daughter's divorce, he was so desperate that he devised a very simple solution to the problem. He would borrow his buddy's boat, take his son-in-law fishing, and then tie him up and toss him overboard with some concrete overshoes!

Fortunately Harry never enacted his plan, and today Harry feels quite differently about the whole situation. "I never would have thought it," he says, "but the divorce was the best thing that ever happened to my daughter. She was always withdrawn, uninvolved, and seemed very unhappy. And I never realized the pressure that she was living under. When her husband left her, she was devastated at first, but she's gotten a job and become more self-confident. I see her now as a much happier and more fulfilled woman than she ever was in her marriage."

Accepting Your Child as Single Again

As mentioned in the section on bargaining, the older generation was raised to believe that you "don't belong to anyone" until you are married. A corollary belief is that parents are responsible for their children until they are married. But what happens when your adult child becomes single again?

What often happens is that mom and dad fall back into those feelings of responsibility. Mothers may feel that their sons aren't eating right or can't do their laundry. Many dads feel responsible for making sure their adult daughter goes to church or that her car is running all right. But part of acceptance is coming to the realization that, "My child is fine as a single and doesn't have to have anyone to take care of him or her."

It may be difficult to accept the fact that your son or daughter may never remarry. He or she may choose to remain single or may never find "Ms. or Mr. Right." Similarly, your daughter (or your son, for that matter) may opt to raise your grandchildren alone as a single parent. This may not be ideal, but acceptance means that you will encourage and support this lifestyle as well.

Contentment

Genuine acceptance is based on contentment—contentment with your family as it is today, not how you envision it in the future or the way it was in the past. Contentment means learning to settle in with the lifestyle of your child, the visitation you have with your grandchildren, and the changes that have come to characterize your family. Don't live with a mindset that focuses on *someday*—someday it will be better, someday this will change, someday there will be justice. So long as you are living for tomorrow, you have not accepted the situation as it is.

Acceptance means turning the present details of your life and of your family life over to God, and then resting. Even though this is not what you would have chosen, it is reality; you can rest in the care of God because He knows what is best for you and how to take care of you. And God can help you learn to be content wherever you find yourself to be.

Making the Journey

Until you "arrive" at acceptance, give yourself permission to be on a journey. It's all right to admit that you are on the road to acceptance but that you're not there yet. Even when you get there, remember that acceptance doesn't mean that you will never have doubts or regrets. On the contrary, chances are good that you will slide back down the slippery slope again.

Remember that the reason we call it a "slippery slope" is that it's like an emotional roller coaster. Something will happen, and you'll find yourself thinking, "Boy! If only he hadn't left!" or "If only she had tried harder to work things out!" You may slide right back down through the stages of grief.

The difference now, however, is that you won't stay long in any of those stages because you have been learning and working through them. Acceptance never means that you will live happily ever after! But what it does mean is that, in your heart, you have a settled, peaceful sense that "This is still my family. We can still be close and we can still show a lot of love for one another."

FORGIVENESS

One mother admitted freely, "I hold grudges. That is just my nature. I hold grudges longer than most people." Even though several years have passed since her son married "the other woman," this mother says, "I just can't forgive her."

This scenario is not unusual. Perhaps you share this struggle. Just now you feel that the divorce has shattered your son or daughter beyond repair. Family life will never be the same. Your heart breaks at the thought of your grandchildren and all that they face as a result of the divorce of their parents. Wrongs have been done; sins have been committed. There is anger, disappointment, and pain. You have a "right" to be bitter!

You can choose to be bitter. But think about it. Bitterness ties you up in knots. Bitterness hurts you far more than it hurts anyone else. It keeps you from living a happy, productive life. It hardly touches the other person. Yes, you can choose to be bitter. Or you can choose something better.

Handling Bitterness

We can handle bitterness in many ways. The worst possible way is to decide it isn't there. The best possible way is to look at it for what it is: Recognize it, identify it, and decide to get rid of it. You say, "Great! How do I do that?" Look at what Paul said to the Ephesians: "Let all bitterness, wrath, anger, clamor, and evil speaking be put away from you, with all malice. And be kind to one another, tenderhearted, forgiving one another, even as God in Christ forgave you" (Eph. 4:31–32).

Better Than Bitter

Did you ever see that snooty ad that boasted, "Living well is the best revenge?" Here's a new wrinkle on that adage: The best revenge is not revenge at all, but forgiveness. Why is that? Romans 12:21 says, "Do not be overcome by evil, but overcome evil with good." Bitterness is an evil response to evil things. A bitter attitude is never helpful. It just allows you to be "overcome by evil." It can hurt your health, your relationships, and your work, among other things. Forgiveness, on the other hand, allows you to regain control of your emotions. It helps you to win, to overcome.

A dictionary definition of the word *forgive* is "to give up resentment against or the desire to punish; stop being angry with; pardon" or "to give up all claim to punish or exact penalty for an offense." What does this mean? And how do we apply it to our situation?

Some teachers encourage the offended party to absorb the

pain and release the offender. Others urge those who are hurt to simply turn to God and confess. Then God will resolve the pain, and everything will be fine. A third approach says that those unable to forgive should examine their own lives. They should see what mistakes they've made—even if the mistake is carrying pain from those who harmed them—and seek forgiveness from those they can't seem to forgive.

These approaches contain certain elements of healthy forgiveness, but they present only part of the forgiveness process. They leave out basic steps that must take place for forgiveness to be authentic and complete. The Bible teaches that there are two sides to God's forgiveness: a legal side and a relational side. Taken together, they form a pattern that teaches us how to forgive one another.

Forgiving One Another Legally

The legal aspect of forgiveness must be addressed before dealing with relational issues. That is, it is essential to be squared away with God to be able to mend relationships on the human level.

Forgiveness begins with an understanding of our legal position before God. The Bible teaches that God, who is holy and righteous, can legally accept only perfect people. However, we can't live perfect lives! Since we have broken God's laws, a penalty must be paid.

The good news is that Jesus Christ lived a perfect life. He is the only person who ever deserved acceptance by God. By His death, He willingly paid the penalty for our failures. He offered His perfect life to be credited to our account, to pay our debt to God. We can be considered legally perfect by God, since the penalty we deserved has been paid by Christ, in accordance with what God's law required.

With that in mind, return to Ephesians 4:32. It says, "forgiving one another, *even as God in Christ forgave you*" (emphasis added). So, why should we forgive? Because we ourselves have been forgiven by God. Legally, we are declared "not guilty" before God because of what Christ did on the cross. Jesus Himself told a parable that illustrates this very well.

Imagine that you are praying. And while you're praying, God brings to your mind the bitter feelings that you have toward those who have hurt you and your loved ones as the separation and divorce have unfolded. You know that before God, you are like the unforgiving servant in Matthew 18. Jesus died on the cross to forgive you, and yet you haven't been willing to forgive those who have wronged you. Remember, the unmerciful slave had forgotten about his own debt. He focused only on the debt owed to him. In the same way, when you get caught up in feelings of anger toward others, you forget your own condition before God and what it took for Him to forgive you.

Mark 11:25 says, "Whenever you stand praying, if you have anything against anyone, forgive him, that your Father in heaven may also forgive you your trespasses." We must do business with God before we do business with anyone else. We must remember the depth of the forgiveness He has extended to us and consider the problem we have with another as a few dollars in comparison to the problem we had with God.

When we go before God and deal with our own attitudes and feelings, we are humbled before Him. Our bitterness is resolved. The result is what the Bible calls a *gentle spirit*. If in our

......................ps we exhibit a gentle spirit, we can focus on the real issues relationally.

As forgiven people, we can, and must, forgive.

Forgiving One Another Relationally

It's really hard to talk to someone with whom we have a problem! Few of us enjoy conflict. But so long as we avoid the real issues we will feel relational pain and anger. We must extend forgiveness to those with whom we are out of relationship just as God has offered forgiveness to us. But that doesn't mean we just forgive and act as if nothing has happened.

A breakdown in a relationship demands an honest dealing with the facts and feelings involved. Take a second look at the Matthew passages first mentioned in Chapter 2.

> *Matthew 5:23–24:* "Therefore if you bring your gift to the altar, and there remember that *your brother has something against you,* leave your gift there before the altar, and go your way. First be reconciled to your brother, and then come and offer your gift" (emphasis added).

> *Matthew 18:15:* "Moreover, *if your brother sins against you,* go and tell him his fault between you and him alone. If he hears you, you have gained your brother" (emphasis added).

As mentioned earlier, whether someone has something against you (see Matt. 5), or whether you have something against another person (see Matt. 18), the responsibility to seek reconciliation is always yours! We are to take the initiative in restoring relationships, just as God took the initiative when He sent His son.

Taking the initiative means going to the person, sharing your perception of the problem, and seeking clarification of your understanding. You must listen to the response of the other person and be willing to hear any new evidence. Your motive is to help both of you recognize the problem that exists and do something about it.

When Not to Forgive

Jesus said, "If your brother sins against you, rebuke him; and if he repents, forgive him." The words, "if he repents, forgive him" challenge our stereotyped idea of forgiveness. With those words, Christ put a condition on forgiveness. He said that *if the person repents,* forgive him.

We already read in Mark 11:25 and Matthew 18:15 that if we have something against a person, we're to forgive him. Did Jesus contradict Himself?

There are two sides of forgiveness. On the legal side, we must deal with our attitude before God. On the relational side, we approach our brother or sister with humility to discuss our problem. But, what if the person we need to reconcile with refuses to admit that there is a problem? Or even worse, what if he sees what he has done but won't accept his share of responsibility for the broken relationship?

When a relationship remains unresolved, there is still pain. And we must recognize that it is still broken. And in such a case, no relational forgiveness has taken place, nor can take place. When the other person recognizes the problem and genuinely asks forgiveness—that is, repentance takes place—we are to genuinely forgive him. His repentance and our forgiveness bring closure to the problem—reconciliation—and newness to the relationship.

We must also look at ourselves. Repairing a broken relationship usually involves both parties asking for forgiveness since problems are rarely so one-sided. We need to be willing to examine our part in the disagreement, and if warranted, go to the other person to initiate the reconciliation process.

Forgiveness *doesn't* mean that everything will go back to the way it was. Nor does it mean that we easily forget what has happened. But it *does* mean that we no longer have a desire to get even or even ask God to zap him. Forgiveness is saying from the heart, "I wish her well. I mourn over what happened, but I no longer harbor hatred or resentment toward her."

FACING THE FUTURE

Forgiving the past doesn't mean that we won't get angry in the future for future hurts. When an ex-son-in-law doesn't follow through with child support payments or an ex-daughter-in-law hurts the children, we get angry all over again.

The truth is that divorce goes on and on. It's a lifetime experience, especially when there are children involved. There will be proms and graduations, birthdays, and maybe even a remarriage in your adult child's future. Each event provides an opportunity for new hurts. But in acceptance we deal with each issue as it comes up. We don't deal with new issues with an old attitude: "I forgave him, but he's late again—this time for his daughter's graduation! Well, that's typical." Dredging up all the old stuff is not forgiveness! Forgiveness means letting go of all the old stuff and dealing with each new issue from a position of peace.

PART II

*Relating to Your Child
After Divorce*

5

Family Secrets

Men stumble over the truth from time to time, but most pick themselves up and hurry off as if nothing had happened.

—Sir Winston Churchill

"We never thought it would end like this," Marie admitted sadly. "John and Pat were devoted to each other. They had such a good relationship—it was a shock." Had Marie's husband, Peter, ever suspected, even for a moment, that his son's marriage might not work out? "Absolutely not!" he said. What had made him so confident that this marriage would last? "It was John's commitment to spiritual things."

No wonder Marie and Peter were so distressed to discover that their son, John, a respected church elder and the father of five, was having an affair. To Marie and Peter's grief, John's affair paved the way to the breakup of his marriage. Along with the pain of losing what had, to them, been an ideal family, Marie and Peter discovered something that deeply disturbed them: Their son not only defended his adultery but also was willing to sacrifice his family and his reputation to continue in it. Six years after their son's divorce, Peter and Marie still shake their heads in amazement that something like this could have

49

happened in their family. "We had such high hopes for John," said his disappointed dad.

Like Marie and Peter, many parents have been unpleasantly surprised to learn the story behind their son or daughter's divorce. Most of the time, parents are unaware of the intimate details of their children's personal lives. That is, most sons and daughters are uncomfortable disclosing to their parents the sordid details of their marital problems, or blow-by-blow descriptions of their last fight. When parent and child are especially close and details are shared, the disclosures regarding divorce may not be that surprising. Most parents, however, find themselves asking, "How could we *not* have known? They seemed so happy. We thought they were the ideal couple."

As part of his doctoral dissertation, in 1989, Thomas Bartlett, Ph.D., surveyed 168 divorcing individuals to discover their reasons for splitting up with their mates. The survey revealed that 75 percent of the respondents attributed their divorces to one of four problems. In order of highest to lowest incidence, these were:

1. Infidelity
2. Desertion
3. Substance abuse (mostly alcohol, some drug use)
4. Physical, sexual, or emotional abuse.

According to this research, most divorces stem from extremely difficult and painful marital circumstances. It stands to reason, then, that the majority of parents whose children divorce will also be faced with difficult or shocking truths about the couple

involved. When your own flesh and blood has done something
that goes against everything you stand for, how do you react?

INFIDELITY

As Dr. Bartlett's survey indicates, infidelity is a growing
problem among both men and women. The fact that extramar-
ital affairs are on the increase, however, does not lessen the
emotional devastation left in their wake. The discovery that
one's son or daughter has had or is having a sexual liaison outside of marriage can be terrible news. Many parents are plunged
into feelings of guilt, anger, depression, or a desire to somehow
fix the situation.

While all of these reactions are quite normal, it is important to keep in mind that you had nothing to do with your
child's decision to "cheat," and you will have very little to do
with the way the affair eventually affects the marriage. Once
infidelity comes to light, parental advice usually has little effect. Still it is well-advised for parents to have one serious conversation with their child about how they feel about the
situation. The conversation should go something like this but
above all, be from the heart.

"Your mother and I are very disturbed about this new person in your life. We believe that this relationship is wrong.
We are trying not to judge you, and we realize that we
don't know everything you went through in your marriage.
Still, no matter how bad it might have become, we can't
condone this response. We would like to see you end this
relationship immediately, and take steps to restore your
marriage. We know this will be very difficult, but we be-

lieve that with God's help, some good counsel, and ade-
quate time, you and (your spouse) can overcome this, and
even use it to begin building a better relationship."

Once you've said your piece, and fully expressed how you
feel, then let your son or daughter know that you will not raise
this issue again. Let them know that you will always be open to
talk, but that you will understand if they choose not to discuss
it further. This may be a very difficult resolution to abide by!
However, this is truly your son or daughter's problem, not your
own. If she is going to work through it, she must decide to do
so on her own, and she must find her own help. You may offer
the name of a pastor or counselor, but don't schedule the ap-
pointment or offer to take her. She must take full personal responsibility for such an important step.

Forced behavior change (in adults) is rarely effective. A
person must come to his own conclusion that what he is doing
is wrong and that he must change. It may be a while before he
suffers the consequences of his actions.

Be emotionally prepared to allow your son or daughter to
make his or her own choices, to experience the pain that results from those choices, and then be prepared as well to be
there when the child comes to her senses.

How will your child's infidelity affect your relationship?
There will definitely be an impact on the parent-child relationship, so consider all aspects of the situation carefully, and discuss with your spouse appropriate responses. The best course of
action is neither to punish your child nor to support the infidelity. Working this out in practical terms can be very sticky!
With your spouse, consider the following:

- Will we help financially?
- Will we let our son or daughter move in with us?
- Will we limit topics of discussion? (For example, "You're not to mention [the partner's] name in this house.")
- Will we allow him to bring his girlfriend over on Christmas Eve?
- How will we treat our daughter-in-law?
- What will we say to our grandchildren about their father's behavior?

These and many other questions must be answered. It is important that you and your spouse discuss how you will respond, and then explain your decisions to your child, and if appropriate, to his spouse. If you are caught off guard by an unexpected question from them, feel free to ask for time to think things over. It's better to take your time and work through your emotions, than to respond in haste and say something you will regret.

It is important that your relationship with your son or daughter continue, even though the nature of the relationship may have to change.

What If the Infidelity Is with Someone of the Same Sex?

For many parents, the discovery that their child's infidelity has been a homosexual affair can make the experience even more shocking and painful. But, once again, it is important not to get bogged down with self-incrimination. Many parents in this situation obsess on their parenting, events from the past, and their own wrongdoing as a way of explaining why their child has turned out this way. The truth is that it is almost impossible to find a direct cause for homosexual behavior.

You may find it more difficult to speak with your child about a homosexual affair, but it is still essential to have the same loving, confrontative talk with your child. Even though you may find it hard to understand the lifestyle, it is best to try to extend the same balance of nonjudgmental love, while refusing to support or condone the behavior.

DESERTION

A spouse rarely runs off for no reason, even if he or she runs off with another person. (Such cases are perhaps more accurately classified as infidelity.) On the other hand, some people say they have been deserted because their spouse moved into another bedroom.

The issue of desertion can be very complex. The question, "Who deserted whom?" is always difficult. To simplify discussion, we will define desertion to have occurred when one partner physically, emotionally, and/or financially abandons all responsibility to the other person. As a parent, how you might be of help will depend on a number of circumstances.

What If Your Son Deserts Your Daughter-in-Law?

Helping Your Son

The first step in this kind of situation is to be willing to listen to your son's reasons for leaving. Then discuss the problem privately with your spouse and decide if you can support your son in his decision and if you are willing to help. If so, to what extent? What if your son wants to move in with you? What if he needs financial help?

If you as a couple decide that you can't support his decision or can't offer help, make your feelings clear to him and urge him to return to his family and work through the problems. Apart from offering the name of a good counselor, resist the temptation to make things too easy for him. If your son has deserted his wife and children, you need to be prepared for the fact that he may desert you too. This could mean borrowing money and leaving town, or ending the relationship as soon as you disagree with him.

If you do agree with your son's reasons for leaving his wife, make sure you don't condone his abandoning his children. He needs to stay in close contact with them and must support them financially. Failing to do so is not only criminal; the neglect will also come back to haunt him later in several ways. Financial abandonment of one's children usually inflicts physical hardship on the children, strains the father-child relationship, and damages the father's credit rating.

Helping Your Daughter-in-Law or Son-in-Law

If you cannot support your son in his move, next you must decide if you will then support your daughter-in-law. If she has children and has been abandoned physically and financially, I would encourage you to do all you can to help her. Financial help may be her most obvious need, but you are probably limited in how much you can provide. However, you do have an abundant supply of love and encouragement.

If it is your son-in-law who has been deserted by your daughter, then these same principles would apply. While this is a lot less frequent, I recently became involved in two cases where each wife left her husband and children to pursue a "new love." In both cases, the parents and in-laws were very involved in helping the men manage their homes and children.

What If It Is My Son or Daughter Who Is Deserted?

Once again, be willing to listen to your adult child and then discuss privately with your spouse how much to help. Although there are always two sides to every story, in a case of true abandonment, it is critical for you to support your child fully at this time.

What If My Daughter Deserts Her Husband and Children?

While this situation occurs less frequently, it does happen. More typically a daughter takes the children and wants to move in with her parents or another friend.

What should you do in such a case? In a crisis, you should probably take your daughter in immediately. It is vital at that point for you and your spouse to discuss privately exactly how much help you will provide and where the limits will be set. It is important that you and your spouse be of one accord. Help from a third party, such as a counselor or a pastor, may be extremely helpful in making these very difficult decisions.

Rarely will a woman abandon all and leave her family unless she is involved in another relationship, drug-addicted, or mentally unstable. You may have no choice in such cases but to stay out of the problem. If you do have contact with your daughter, certainly encourage her to get help and perhaps offer to help her get it.

ADDICTION

Dealing with an adult child's infidelity or abandonment involves similar guidelines. Namely, the parents can feel free to express their feelings of concern and then, no matter how painful it may be, they must avoid trying to control the life of their child. But when addiction is involved, those guidelines no longer apply. An alcohol- or drug-addicted person is truly in bondage to a substance and will not seek help on his own. In cases of addiction, you need to intervene in your adult child's life. (For further information see the Recommended Reading and Resources at the end of this book.)

The most common addictions are to substances—alcohol and (illegal or prescription) drugs. But addiction can take many forms. People can also become addicted to gambling, spending, and sex. All of these behaviors move the family toward divorce and the individual toward self-destruction. You may need to intervene as a family (again, with professional help). The goal is to save the person, or to at least save the rest of your family, before reaching the point of physical, emotional, or financial ruin.

ABUSE

Gregory was a pastor who did not believe in divorce under any circumstances. He took a very rigid stand on this issue and counseled many couples to "hang in there and work it out." But the day that he learned his own daughter was being battered by her husband, Gregory found a different response

...ing up inside of him. He took swift action and helped his daughter move out of her home immediately.

Gregory readily admits that he is now very confused about the issue, but he is not apologetic about his actions. "I just couldn't stand by and allow my daughter to be abused. My pastoral instincts were put on hold and my fatherly instincts took over," he explained.

As parents, you may or may not want to give advice concerning whether or not your children divorce. But in the case of abuse, do not hesitate to exercise your parental instincts by helping your son or daughter out of a dangerous situation. In the case of abuse, a time of separation is critical.

The separation should be maintained to break the cycle of abuse while both parties seek counseling. For the abuser, there must be a sincere desire to change and then concrete evidence that there has been progress—not words, but behavioral change, borne out over time. Many abusers send cards and flowers of apology and make all kinds of promises but do not change the way they handle their anger. For example, how do they react when they don't get their way? What do they do when the abused partner stands up to them? Genuine change requires time and patience. An abusive man or woman will not change the patterns of relating without outside help and lots of work.

For the person who has been abused, the focus in counseling should be on how he or she contributed to or enabled the abusive cycle. Abuse victims need guidance concerning how to be more assertive and stand strong against any kind of effort to control or manipulate them. This kind of personal growth is helpful whether or not they ever return to their spouse. In my book *Love Gone Wrong*, I outline many examples of abused individuals who tend to leave one abusive relationship merely to enter another. This relational pattern needs to be broken before the person considers entering a new relationship.

Types of Abuse

There are several kinds of abuse. We most commonly think of physical abuse, but there is also sexual abuse (of the spouse and/or the children) and emotional abuse. Actually, emotional abuse is the most common and can be the most damaging. Just about every couple engages in some heated arguments, name calling, and occasional yelling at one another, but that is very different from the cold, calculated emotional abuse that some spouses inflict on their partner or their children.

When there is an accusation of emotional abuse, the truth can be very elusive. Naturally, your instinct is to side with your own child. The best approach is to listen to your child, offer support, and if you can, encourage him or her in the marriage. Suggest, as well, professional help in sorting out what to do. Both you and your child are probably not objective in this matter, and a third party can be quite helpful.

Whatever the type of abuse, don't be surprised if the problem seems to linger and your child remains ambivalent about leaving the spouse. Be prepared for the fact that they may leave and return time and time again against your wishes. Sometimes abuse victims feel that the abusive relationship is the best they can get. Or, they may feel that they deserve the abuse. Some reason that an abusive marriage is better than having no one. Others want to avoid becoming a burden to their parents. Because of the fickle nature of these situations, be careful how strongly you denounce your child's mate. I have seen many a parent join in railing against a spouse only to find their child later vigorously defending the abusive partner.

If your child is not aware of the various helping agencies in the area, help her or him to find this information, especially if you the parent do not live close enough to provide a safe haven. A person in a potentially abusive situation needs to know:

- How to call the police quickly
- How to obtain a restraining order
- Where the local support shelter is located
- Where counseling services are available.

6

Family Boundaries

Love your neighbor, yet pull not down your hedge.
—George Herbert

Recently, my friend Tom Jones and I were speakers at a conference. He spoke early in the day on the subject of *unconditional love*. I spoke later in the day on *relationship boundaries*. Tom gave an excellent talk, as he usually does, on the biblical concept of love, delving into the Greek words and so on. "Unconditional love," he said, "looks for nothing in return, but gives, gives, gives."

In the hours following his talk, both he and I were beset by people saying, "I *did* give, give, give to my spouse and my kids, and now I have nothing left to give. I feel totally used up and worn out. How can I go on and still get nothing in return?"

I quickly realized that these people needed to hear my talk about boundaries!

Unconditional love and boundaries go hand in hand. That is, love must be balanced with limits and boundaries, and these two concepts must be understood in tandem.

Unconditional love is a *personal* ideal. As an individual,

61

you need to offer love with no selfish strings attached. Otherwise, it's not love but manipulation or bargaining. Jesus made this point as he urged people to love their enemies. "For if you love those who love you, what reward have you? Do not even the tax collectors do the same?" (Matt. 5:46). The tax collectors were viewed as the vilest of people. (Imagine that!)

But in a relationship, new rules enter the picture. Suddenly I must be concerned not only with you and me, but with us. I may live my life in a self-giving, undemanding, sacrificial way, but for a relationship to work, the love has to flow both ways. For the good of us, I must require you to show love to me as well. That takes boundaries.

The poet Robert Frost was onto something profound when he wrote, "Good fences make good neighbors" ("Mending Wall"). We tend to think that everything in a relationship should be free and giving: no closed doors, no holding back, no saying no. We don't like walls, but they're necessary for good relationships. And good fences make healthy family relationships.

Any relationship within a family is a three-legged stool—me, you, and "it"—the relationship. If we lose ourselves, if we don't know who we are, if the relationship becomes exclusively about one person—the stool collapses. All three elements are necessary. How can you ensure that all three elements will be strong? You need to protect your own self, empower the other person, and define your role.

PROTECTING YOURSELF

Picture this: A person walks inside on a hot day, takes a pitcher of water out of the refrigerator and pours it—all over the kitchen table. Without a glass to hold it, the water is useless for quenching thirst. It's all over the place. The water needs *boundaries*.

So it is with a "liquid" person. Some people pour themselves out for others, particularly their family. They lose all sense of who they are. Their identity is wrapped up in the lives of others. They have no boundaries. Sad to say, those people are like the water dripping onto the kitchen floor. Without those personal boundaries, they can't do much good, even for the people they're pouring themselves out for.

How do you know if you lack personal boundaries? Symptoms include the following:

- Inability to say "no" to others
- Being overly involved in your son or daughter's personal life
- Knowing intimate secrets
- Thinking about your son or daughter's problems all the time while neglecting your own responsibilities
- Dreading your involvement in the whole mess
- Feeling burned out and drained
- Running yourself ragged for someone else's sake
- Neglecting your spouse or your other children
- Letting others determine how you feel
- Doing all the work to find friends, housing or a job for your child while she shows little motivation to do anything for herself.

There is a big difference between being responsible *for* your children and being responsible *to* your children. When children are small and dependent, parents are responsible *for* them.

The parent, not the child, must see that the child eats a balanced diet, wears warm clothes in the winter, and treats pets and playmates properly. If the child is sick, the responsibility is the parent's to get the child to the doctor. Parents are responsible to train a child to use the bathroom, to say "please" and "thank you" and to clean his room.

As the child grows, he is able to take more and more responsibility for his own physical needs, his own decisions, and his own problems. By the time they are grown, children are, by definition, *adults*—they are old enough to make their own decisions, be responsible for their own finances, their own relationships, and their own problems.

Perhaps the greatest disservice a parent can do to an adult child is to continue to be responsible for her. Parents who feel responsible for their grown child continue to rescue him from pain, from mistakes, and from difficult relationships. Indeed, part of the reason some adult children seem to never learn from their mistakes is that someone always steps in and shields them from the consequences of their choices. Parents who bail a child out of jail, pay off the credit cards, mediate between the spouses, and quit their jobs to take care of their grandchildren only guarantee that they will be forever cast in the role of rescuing parent! In reality, pain, past due notices, and relational problems can be wonderful tutors if parents do not deprive their child of the opportunity to learn from them.

EMPOWERING YOUR CHILDREN

Loving your children unconditionally while maintaining proper boundaries is the way to be responsible *to* and not *for* your children. This combination of love and boundaries *empowers* your children. Empowering is the alternative to enabling.

Instead of enabling your child to continue in unproductive ways, seek to empower him or her to learn new lessons and become better through this crisis of divorce or separation. Empowering happens not through excuses but encouragement; not through forgive and forget but forgive and learn; not through "I love you and I don't care what you do" but loving accountability. Empowering looks something like this:

- Being compassionate but not feeding his self-pity
- Being generous but expressing your own expectations
- Listening but also letting her know how you feel
- Offering advice but not lecturing
- Being available to help but not making the decisions for her.

Empowering rather than enabling is difficult, because it is hard for any parent to sit by during a time of failure for his child. But healthy boundaries mean you will have to do that. You will not be able to save your child when he or she makes poor choices. If the parent-child relationship becomes all about teaching your child how to act, what to say, and what to do next, you're losing balance. That's enabling and not empowering.

Parents with a clear sense of boundaries understand that while they can be available to their child, offering love, time, and a shoulder to cry on, the child's problems belong to the child, not the parent. Healthy boundaries allow parents to offer money, assistance, child care, food or shelter, but the parent does not exhaust himself and all of his resources to meet the needs of the child. The child must be responsible for himself to a larger degree than the parent is.

Sometimes your adult child will seem bound for self-destruction. Despite all of your counsel, she will insist on going her own way and doing her own thing. In such cases you have no choice but to let her go. In the counseling world, there is a saying: *Sometimes people have to hit bottom before they will look up.* You may find yourself standing aside, watching your child hurtle downhill. Prayer and patience are all you can offer until he comes to his senses. But this too can be a way for you to empower your child. You love her enough to let her choose to waste her talents, resources, and money. After she falls on her face, just like the prodigal son's father, you can be there to love and support her once more. Not to rescue or enable but to empower that child to be all that God intended.

DEFINING YOUR ROLE

Another important part of setting boundaries is to define your role. One popular speaker on family issues uses a hanging mobile to illustrate the dynamics in any family. He points out that the movement of any one family member affects everyone else significantly, just as when you move one part of the mobile.

When your son or daughter divorces, the family changes and your role in the situation must be redefined. The three most important relationships that need to be reevaluated are the ones with your spouse, your divorcing son or daughter, and your ex in-law. Your relationships with your other children and your grandchildren will also be affected, but to a lesser degree.

Your Relationship with Your Spouse

Even if you already have a good relationship with your spouse, going through a family divorce puts a tremendous strain on it. Any weaknesses will be magnified, and weak relationships can themselves easily be turned toward divorce.

Most couples find themselves disagreeing on some aspect of their adult child's divorce. Therefore, as mentioned earlier, you need to confer with your spouse on these issues and decide *together* what your role and response will be. Be aware that not only is this important for the well-being of your adult child, your own marriage is being subjected to an overwhelming weight of strain and stress. You need time for the two of you to work out disagreements, hurts, or expectations with each other.

Your Relationship with Your Child

Your adult child will probably grow more dependent on you during this crisis. For years you felt secure about his marriage and assumed he was well taken care of. Now suddenly, he seems to need you as much as when he was in your care—more so if there are children involved. Your adult child may seek you out for advice, money, child care, or emotional support. Many parents describe feeling responsible for their child for years following divorce, often until there is remarriage.

Whether you're male or female, we all need emotional support, companionship, a listening ear, and a little TLC once in a while. When hit with divorce, family and close friends often move in close to fill that void, particularly in the beginning.

The parent-child relationship can grow closer as a result of divorce. But what if it goes the other way? You may feel anger, disappointment, shame, or a whole host of other negative emotions toward your child. Perhaps he did not follow your advice or example, and his life is now in shambles as a result of his own belligerence.

Anger or resentment is quite normal, but taking it out on her right now is not going to prove helpful. Your child will probably distance herself from you, and you may lose her for years. While you may be right about the mistakes, the time to work and make improvements in character will come later. For now, hold your hostility and try to nurture instead. Choose wisely the one time to speak your mind, but remember she may be too depressed or rebellious to hear your counsel, let alone act on it.

Consider this analogy. If your child were in intensive care due to a massive heart attack, you might be mad at him for not exercising, not eating properly, or not taking care of himself. But you wouldn't run to the hospital to give him a "good piece of your mind" or pull him out of bed in order to start a new exercise program.

The same is true in divorce. For now you need to be there for him. You don't want your child to look back and think, "The one time I needed my parents the most, they were too angry to help me."

Your Relationship with Your Ex-Son- or Daughter-in-Law

Your relationship with the estranged spouse will be much more difficult to manage and complicated to maintain than any other in a divorce. Other than occasional visits with the grandchildren, it is unusual for these relationships to continue for very long after the divorce. If you're like most parents, once you tried to make your new son-in-law or daughter-in-law a part of the family. The departure will leave a big void in your life and start a painful grieving process.

Part of your setting healthy new boundaries in this relationship is to discuss with your own child your relationship with the ex. In most cases you will be encouraged to "do whatever you want," but you must determine over time what that really means. You may discover that it translates, "When you see the jerk, I don't want to hear about it." Or it may mean, "Did you see him/her this week? Tell me all about it!"

Finding a relationship with your ex-in-law that works in the context of your enduring relationship with your own child may be difficult, but it is important. You should neither be a messenger nor a mediator between your child and the former mate.

Sometimes your child will insist that you have no relationship with the ex-spouse. This may be very difficult, or it may be a relief. You will need to decide with your own spouse how to respond to this request, and then be honest with your own child about what you will do. Sneaking around in order to maintain a relationship with an ex-in-law or your grandchildren will only further hurt everyone involved.

In reality, most cases where a relationship with the ex-in-law is maintained involve the custodial parent (usually the wife) bringing the grandchildren over for occasional visits. One woman says, "I used to really look forward to the visits with my daughter-in-law. She used to bring the kids over once in a while for the afternoon. We'd just sit and visit, getting updated on each others lives and how the children were doing in school. She'd never ask about our son though, and I'd never offer. After about three years, she remarried. He sounded like a wonderful man, but then our relationship dwindled. I guess there was no room in their new family for an ex-mother-in-law."

It is fairly typical for these relationships to ebb over time. This is especially true when either your child or your ex-in-law remarries. Most remarried couples want to set new boundaries that will ensure the success of the new marriage. These boundaries many times start with walls in the relationships with the former spouse and his or her family.

You will, however, want to maintain a relationship with your grandchildren no matter what the circumstances. If your child is the noncustodial parent, you may find that this will be increasingly through phone calls and letters. As the grandchildren are older and begin to drive, they may choose to come and visit once in a while.

Guidelines for the New Roles

When you think about defining these three relationships (your spouse, your child, and your former in-law), you might want to consider the following guidelines.

1. Talk with the other person about the relationship you share. Start by asking what he or she wants from you in this relationship. The other party may not know right now his needs, but your request will at least encourage him to think and perhaps establish new boundaries.

2. Discuss with the other person what you need. What are your expectations, limits, and boundaries? Evaluate those needs objectively to be sure your requests are reasonable.

3. Decide what you expect from the relationship and what you're willing to give. Whether it's your child, your ex-in-law, or someone else, think carefully about your expectations, your limits, and how much of yourself and your resources you're willing to give. Once you make these decisions, resist the urge to resent people who need or want more than you can provide. Then simply say *no* when asked to go beyond what you're willing to do.

4. If necessary, draw up an agreed set of rules for the relationship. This is critical if the other person will be moving in with you or borrowing money. If your relationship is already in pretty good shape, the communication required by the first three steps may be enough. But if things must change, agree together on the terms of your relationship.

5. Be ready to pull out if the rules are not followed. Decide in advance: one strike? Two strikes? Three? How important are those rules to you? Are you willing to hold firm to these relationship boundaries? Or how much flexibility should there be?

6. Be aware that some relationships may not survive. In most divorces there are significant losses. You may have to face the loss of an important relationship in your life: an in-law, the other parents, perhaps even your grandchildren or your own child. This may not seem right or fair, but in many cases it might be a hard reality. If you hold to certain boundaries, others may attempt to push you well beyond your limits. It may be painful, but for the relational health of all concerned, it is important to hold to your convictions.

It's possible that the other person will respond to your firm stand. You may, in time, restore your relationship on healthy, equitable terms. And that, of course, would be best.

BOUNDARIES VS. LIMITS: A TEST CASE

Sometimes you bend and stretch your boundaries as far as you can and then finally reach your limit. Using the liquid analogy from the beginning of the chapter, boundaries are the container that keeps you from spilling all over the place. A plastic bag will flex when pushed on (sometimes the boundaries will be stretched), but not break. Limits, however, are better represented by a brick—a velvet-covered brick.

When people push on your boundaries and you must say *no*, having limits is what causes you to stand firm. The velvet is there to soften the blow. Instead of responding to an unreasonable request with, "No, and I don't want to hear anymore about it!" you can say, "I'd love to help out, but I just can't do that."

Setting limits is similar to setting boundaries: You must decide ahead of time where you will be flexible and where you will draw your lines. Most lines are drawn along the issues of money, kids, and housing. Take a look at this example.

Paul and Casey's marriage got off to a bad start. They had very little money, a small efficiency apartment, and Casey was pregnant. Since Casey was very close to her mother, she tended to tell her everything that was going on in the marriage, calling her sometimes three or four times a day. As Paul and Casey's marital stress increased, the length and frequency of the calls to her mother increased. It did not take long before Paul started to resent the calls and blamed his mother-in-law for intruding on their marriage.

As Casey turned more and more to her mother for support, Paul felt increasingly isolated and started drinking more and more. At first it was four or five beers a night; soon he said it wasn't worth coming home until late because Casey would just be on the phone with her mother.

The powder keg was finally lit one night when Paul came home late and drunk. Casey complained about his condition and Paul struck her in the ensuing fight. Without hesitation Casey grabbed some things and left for her mother's. By now she was eight months pregnant.

By the next morning Mr. and Mrs. Keating had agreed to a compromise position: Casey was welcome to stay, but she must get neutral counsel, with or without Paul. They offered to pay for part of the counseling, but left it up to them as to who they would see and whether the goal of counseling would be separation or reconciliation (another healthy boundary).

Paul and Casey entered counseling only weeks before the birth of a beautiful baby boy. The excitement of the new arrival brought them back together, and Paul was very attentive, at least for a while. The Keatings were thrilled.

Casey still called her mother frequently, but Mrs. Keating, at the urging of her husband, encouraged Casey to talk to her husband more and put some boundaries on the topics they discussed. For the next several weeks, with the Keatings' financial help, Paul went to counseling—or so he said. As it turned out, he was using the counseling money to go to a bar and commiserate with his buddies about the trials of having a new baby in the house.

Casey called her mom right away, of course. Mrs. Keating advised Casey to confront Paul on her own, while she discussed the problem with her husband (another boundary).

The counselor recommended an intervention to convince Paul to go into an alcohol rehabilitation center. Paul indicated that he would consider it. The Keatings, with the encouragement of the counselor, requested that Paul pay them back for the money he took for counseling. In addition, they set some new limits. They told him that they could not help him in any way until he went for treatment. They also decided together that they would encourage Casey to stay with Paul, but if she left him, they would help her.

Fortunately, Paul did get treatment and has now been sober for several months. He has set new boundaries for his life, and Casey is working on new boundaries in hers. The Keatings are working together to see that their children succeed, yet they know that they need to stay out of most of their children's personal life and problems. They have also learned some of the limits which, when put into effect, empower their children to cope on their own when the next problem comes up.

7

Family Loyalties

I always felt like my parents were siding with my ex-husband. Whenever they got a chance they seemed to bring him up to me—how nice he was, and how much they missed him. I felt like I was betraying them by insisting on the divorce. I know they felt that I had failed them and failed my marriage.

—*Brenda*

Bob and Wilma had three married children. Their middle child, David, got married during graduate school and asked for ongoing financial help from his parents even after his marriage. He and his new wife, Carol, lived in a condo that Bob and Wilma owned. They charged David and Carol no rent.

After David graduated and started his professional career, he and Carol continued to live in his parents' condo. Bob and Wilma still allowed them to stay there rent-free because they wanted to help the young couple save for a house of their own. Unfortunately, when Carol was six months pregnant, she and David began having severe marital problems. Before their baby was born, David left his wife and moved in with someone else. With her in-law's permission, after the baby was born, Carol and the baby remained in the condo.

Bob and Wilma's greatest dilemma came when their son began to pressure them to reduce their contact with Carol. They were gracious to David, even though they did not agree with his request. For a while, they honored his wishes and lessened their contact with Carol. They wanted to help her more, but agreed that they should stay more neutral, for the sake of their son.

All along, Bob and Wilma had discussed how they should be treating David and Carol. Although it had created a lot of tension between them, they usually agreed that they should support both children emotionally and Carol financially by allowing her to remain in their condo. These boundaries worked well until David raised the ante. He asked his parents to have Carol and the baby leave their condo, so that he and his new girlfriend could move in. "After all," he said, "I need to save money and I'm your flesh and blood. The condo should have been mine all along."

How would you handle this loyalty dilemma?

The Parents' Dilemma

Every divorce has at least two sides. Like Bob and Wilma, as parents you will probably be asked to take one side or the other. Loyalty issues tend to go through two stages, as evidenced by a second look at Bob and Wilma's story.

Stage One

First, during the initial breakup, parents may be asked to choose a side or mediate a dispute. In this beginning stage parents may be able to get away with telling their own son or daughter that they don't agree with what he is doing: He needs to get help, get some sense, or "get real." They encourage the child to go back to his spouse and feel a fierce loyalty to the in-law, as Bob and Wilma did toward Carol. At this point most parents believe that a few adjustments can still turn the marriage around. But when things don't turn around, parents are left with a difficult choice.

Stage Two

While parents may or may not agree with how their child is conducting himself through the crisis, they eventually come to the conclusion, "Right or wrong, this child is still my flesh and blood." Most parents eventually decide that they want to continue a relationship with their son or daughter, no matter what he or she has done. Once parents work through the stages of grieving and arrive at a point of acceptance, the vast majority end up supporting their own child. This sometimes requires the sacrifice of the relationship with the ex-spouse, but other times some kind of relationship can continue.

Let's get back to Bob and Wilma. What did they decide?

For a long time, they agonized over the decision. They even thought about buying another condo, just to avoid having to choose between their son and ex-daughter-in-law. In the end, they decided that they had to support their own son but they could not abandon Carol and their grandchild.

Bob and Wilma told their son in a very loving way that they would not honor his request. Considering Carol's situation, they felt strongly that she should be allowed to stay in the condo until she could afford to move. In addition, they told David that they would continue to love and accept him and that they would continue to accept his new lifestyle.

From that time on, David never asked again about the condo. The relationship is a little strained, but David knows that he is loved by his parents. Carol is beginning to date now, too, so Bob and Wilma feel that they can "back off" a little more. They have let Carol know that as soon as she can afford it, they would prefer that she find a new place to live. They realize that as she moves on with her own life they will need to put more distance between themselves and Carol, but they have vowed to always try to maintain a close relationship with their grandson.

Bob and Wilma are typical in that they eventually decided to prioritize their relationship with their son. They did continue to show kindness and support to their ex-daughter-in-law, however, and eased their relationship with her into a lower gear over an extended period of time. They continue to have a positive relationship with her, which fosters ongoing contact with their grandson. All things considered, Bob and Wilma were able to resolve all of their loyalty conflicts in an ideal way.

SIDING WITH THE IN-LAW

While a majority of parents will eventually choose as Bob and Wilma did, there are exceptions. I interviewed a couple who, in the long run, chose *not* to side with their own child.

The Carluccis

Peggy Carlucci's son and daughter have both divorced. In each case, Peggy and her husband sided with the party they felt was right. When their daughter and son-in-law split up, the Carluccis sided with their own child. "She still loved him," says Peggy, "and did not want the divorce. She couldn't handle him living with another woman while still married to her. We thought she was in the right, so we sided with her."

But when their son left his pregnant wife, Peggy and her husband, Jack, made a different decision. "We were very upset with him. We sided with our daughter-in-law." Almost four years after the divorce, Peggy and Jack remain closer to their former daughter-in-law than to their son. "We still see him; we still talk to him; we still love him. But we do not go to his house," said Jack.

This family situation is an exception to the old adage, "Blood is thicker than water." Sometimes relationships forged by marriage and across the generations are exceptionally durable. They are bonds of the heart and not easily destroyed, even by divorce.

LOYALTY ISSUES

In most families, there are loyalty conflicts of some sort during divorce. These loyalty conflicts are felt across a broad range of issues. Some of the most critical areas of conflict will center on one or more of the following questions.

Who's to Blame?

Human nature always tries to assess blame or figure out why something happened. We may be biased toward our own child and blame the in-law. This type of parent is likely to make statements such as:

"I always knew he was no good."
"We tried to warn him not to marry her."
"It figures. Look at the family she came from."

In the early stages of your child's separation, it is important
to be careful about making these kinds of statements. Say them
if you must to your spouse or to yourself, but refrain from bur-
dening your child with such discouraging comments. Restraint
is in order, of course, because the couple may yet be reconciled,
in which case such statements would be all the more regret-
table. Even if they do not reconcile, both spouses need to hear
encouraging words right now. One thing neither of them needs
to hear is anything that smacks of "I told you so."

Other parents are biased toward their own children with a
negative bias. These parents are quick to blame or think the
worst about their own son or daughter. This sometimes indicates a harsh parenting style or some unresolved parent-child
problem. The comments of these parents might be:

> "My son never listened to me."
> "She didn't learn those behaviors in this house. If only
>   she were a Christian—the way we brought her up."
> "I'm ashamed to admit he's my son."

Once the "Who's to blame?" question is resolved, it is of very
little consequence. No matter who was at fault, all parties suffer
incredible pain. Parents soon realize that finger pointing must be
laid aside if they are to be at all helpful. A more constructive approach says, "Right or wrong, she is our daughter and we must
support her," or "It's hard to admit, but now we know there's really nothing we can do about this. We have to accept the divorce as their decision and move on with our lives."

For many Christians, accepting a divorce is a type of loyalty conflict in itself—a conflict with their own set of values.

Why Can't We Stay Out of It?

Many parents would like to resolve their loyalty problems by staying out of the entire mess of divorce. One parent expressed his frustration: "My son-in-law was like my own son. We went camping together, had many heart-to-heart talks. . . . I felt closer to him than my own daughter. Please don't ask me to take sides."

While the desire to avoid the conflict is understandable, adult children need their parents during divorce and separation more than ever before. The emotional, financial, and spiritual toll is more than one person can handle alone, especially if your child is responsible for her own children. Your adult child may normally be a very stable, responsible parent, but in the midst of a divorce, she can become an easily overwhelmed, emotionally distraught, and very preoccupied parent. For the sake of your children and grandchildren, you must be involved.

Should We Hear the Other Side?

This is a most difficult question, one that is wrought with loyalty pitfalls. While you want to support your own child, you know there are two sides to every story. Would you be disloyal to your child if you sought to hear the other side?

In many cases of divorce, both parties will try to win you over. They may try to get to you in order to get their side aired first. Or they may play the game of constant one-upmanship—putting the spouse down in order to make themselves look better.

If your son-in-law or daughter-in-law seeks you out, you may have no choice but to listen. But it is ill-advised to take the initiative in seeking out the other side of the story without first asking your own child if he or she minds. This can be viewed as a gross betrayal of trust. If your in-law does seek you out and you sense that the motivation is simply to tear down your child, politely ask him to stop.

Why Can't Things Be Fair?

Many divorcing couples, especially those seeking an amicable divorce, start out thinking that everything can be dealt with fairly. That notion lasts only until they get into the real issues of the settlement; then *fair* goes out the window and it's everyone for himself. Parents as well often assume they can approach their children's divorce in a civilized manner and they will deal fairly with all parties.

But divorce always changes the family structure, and it is never fair. Everyone touched by the divorce will be hurt: the marital partners, the children, the couple's parents, and even other siblings, friends, and relatives. If you are a conflict avoider or a peacemaker, you may be in for a surprise. You will probably antagonize both sides and may please no one.

What About the Grandchildren?

Grandchildren are a huge issue in the loyalty debate, and are rightly termed the *innocent victims* of divorce (see Chapters 10—12). Other than your own child, the grandchildren are probably the greatest focus of your attention during a divorce.

But grandchildren are also potentially one of the least controversial loyalty issues. In most families, both parties will appreciate anything you do to help the grandchildren. They may be angry with each other and unable to parent well, but they are able to recognize and be grateful when their children are being helped.

The only time grandchildren become a difficult issue is when there is a custody battle and you are perceived as trying to help or influence only one side of the debate.

As a grandparent, try to focus squarely on what is best for the children. Many times this is different from what is best for the adults. For example, one mother wanted to move back home with her parents, several states away. She had children ranging in age from eight to sixteen, who were adamant about remaining close to their friends, their schools, and their church. When the mother and the grandparents realized that staying would be best for the kids, they came to a resolution and the grandparents were supportive.

It is also important to divide your loyalties equally among your grandchildren. Don't ignore the teens for the sake of the younger kids, or vice versa. Children are never too young not to understand and never get too old not to be hurt. All children suffer in divorce, from infants to those who have already moved on to college or a marriage of their own. Be sympathetic and supportive with all of your grandchildren.

Who Gets the Friends?

Too often, the fate of friends in a divorce is similar to the protocol at a wedding. When you walk into the church, you are asked, "Are you on the bride's or groom's side?" Once you choose, that's where you stay throughout the ceremony.

At worst the two spouses in a divorce can play tug of war, stretching their friends between them and pulling for all they're worth.

In divorces that are more amicable, choosing sides may not be an issue. Neither side would mind if you kept in touch with any of their friends or relatives.

If, as a parent, you've grown close to your children's friends, be prepared for the possible fading of those relationships. In many divorcing situations friends stick close for a period of time, but then all parties move toward people more like them or in similar life circumstances.

What About Relating to My Other Children at This Time?

One last area (which may be common sense, but should be mentioned anyway) is that of considering the feelings and needs of your other children. When one of your children is going through a separation or divorce it is very common for them to need much more of your support and time. But part of balancing loyalty means taking care not to support one child at the expense of the others. Most siblings will be understanding if you are preoccupied for a while but it can create bad blood when that happens for extended periods of time, or whenever there is money involved. Be very sensitive to this issue. Here are a few guidelines.

1. *Make a conscious effort to pursue your other children when their relationship with you is showing signs of strain.* Invite them to dinner, or take them fishing, or just have a heart-to-heart talk with them about how you both are feeling. Look for reasons to just call and chit chat.

2. *While you will probably spend some of your time talking about what is going on with the divorcing child, make sure you don't focus exclusively on that subject.* Ask about what is going on in

the non-divorcing child's life. Be aware that this son or daughter may feel guilty for talking about what seem like petty problems in comparison to divorce: a husband's travel schedule or a child's difficulties at school. If they share a struggle, don't tell them to be thankful that they don't have their sibling's problem! Rather, be sure to communicate that you regard their feelings and their struggles as real and valid.

3. *Watch out when it comes to money.* Communicate with your other children what you are doing for their divorcing sibling and why. Most family secrets don't remain secrets with the other children and only become unspoken resentments. It is better to talk about what you're doing and then perhaps offer some compromise. You might say, "You know your sister is really struggling financially since her husband left, so I want you to know that we are going to be helping her for a while. Once she's back on her feet then maybe we could talk with you about helping with your son's college tuition."

If there is not enough money to extend help to your other adult children, do not hesitate to help your divorcing son or daughter in need anyway. Just explain what you are doing. Most siblings are gracious in such matters when you are honest with them. You may want to arrange things so that it is understood that the money will be paid back when the divorcing child gets on his feet again.

One couple handled their loyalty dilemma this way: When their daughter needed financial help following a divorce, they gave her a substantial loan so that she could keep her home. They told her she could repay it anytime she wanted, if she ever had the money. Then they informed all of their other children about what they had done. In addition, they let them

know that they were writing into their will that their estate
was to be divided equally, and if their divorcing daughter had
any outstanding debt, her portion would be reduced by that
amount.

4. *Be careful about betraying a confidence.* If your divorcing
child is confiding in you specific details and asks you not to tell
the others, honor that request. Let your child know that you
will only discuss general issues with others, but will keep details
in confidence. While open communication is important within
families, a degree of discretion and boundaries is well-advised
when it comes to the details.

Loyalty to your children also means that you don't play one
child against the other, gossip, or show a lack of respect for any
of them. When you disagree with what your child is doing, tell
him or her in a loving way. Then back off. It is indeed possible
to disagree, yet still show respect and support for the person.

8

Providing Emotional Support

God never gives us discernment in order that we may criticize, but that we may intercede.

—*Oswald Chambers*

If there was ever a crisis time in your child's life, this is it! If there was ever a time when your child needed assurance of your love and support, this is it! Shelley, a divorced parent, said, "I can truthfully say that I wish my parents had been closer so they could have put their arms around me. I have never felt *so* alone."

As the mother or father of an adult child experiencing divorce, it is your privilege to encourage your child at this time. You can be an extension of God's love to your child during this crisis. If you will allow yourself to be His eyes, His heart, His arms, His hands, He will use you to touch your child with comfort and encouragement in ways that perhaps no one else will be able to do.

After all, you know your child better than anyone else. You care for this child as only a mother or father can care. You can give encouragement—no matter how you feel about the situation and no matter what your beliefs about divorce—if you focus primarily on your child and the pain he or she is in.

ENCOURAGING YOUR CHILD: YOUR PARENTAL PRIVILEGE

Encouragement takes many forms, but they can be summed up in five categories.

Verbal Encouragement

What you say at this time of crisis can be a lifeline to a child who feels as if she is drowning—drowning in tears, in bills, in responsibilities, in despair. Try to look at things from your child's point of view before you speak: What does he need right now? Proverbs 18:21 says, "Death and life are in the power of the tongue." Words have equal potential for encouragement and discouragement. Words are but tools; how we use them comes from our heart.

Words can either be spoken or written. Spoken words, either by telephone or in person, can express your confidence in your child's ability to make good choices, to cling to God, to make it through the current ordeal. You can point out strengths: your child's sense of humor, intelligence, talents, sensitivity to children, heart for God. Right now, your hurting child needs to hear what's good about himself, what's admirable, what's positive.

Written encouragement—cards, notes, and especially quotations from the Word of God—is enduring. Cards and handwritten notes can be displayed on the refrigerator, a window sill, or a bathroom mirror to dispense encouragement on a daily basis.

Material Encouragement

Sometimes words are not enough. Your son or daughter may need what is basic to survival: food, clothing, or shelter. Your child may be in a financial crisis, unable to pay the rent or buy groceries. Your grandchildren may need dental care, medical care, school clothing, or lunch money.

Divorce especially threatens women and children with economic disaster. Marital breakup is largely responsible for what the media has called "the feminization of poverty." Your daughter or daughter-in-law may need a loan or a gift in order to survive the financial crunch while long-term solutions like affordable housing and stable employment are being pursued.

If survival needs are met, cash and treats "for no reason" can be encouraging because they say, "I love you and I care about you very much."

Tangible Encouragement

Sometimes needs require deeds. A single-again will be profoundly grateful for the friends who help move furniture, care for the yard, drill holes and install appliances, or hang curtains. A single parent will appreciate those who can spend time with his or her child fishing, Christmas shopping, or playing basketball—to fill in the void of male or female leadership. Free baby-sitting can liberate a single parent for some badly needed free time. Divorce requires an increased support system, and parents of the adult child can be key players.

Spiritual Encouragement

One kind of encouragement which every parent can provide is intercessory prayer. When a divorcing person is aware of the fact that Mom and Dad are interceding on their behalf, they are encouraged by the love demonstrated. But most importantly, the life-changing encouragement—the answers to parental prayer—comes from God. Often, parents sense that separation or divorce has weakened or threatens to weaken their child's faith. Because they understand that their child needs God's care and direction now more than ever, they are vigilant in prayer. Joan says, "I think my main concern—and it is a prayer concern—is that my son never leave the Lord. If he did he would be devastated. That would be his ruining [sic]."

James 5:16 says, "The effective fervent prayer of a righteous man avails much." Parents can "avail"—accomplish much—by praying faithfully for their child, their in-law, their grandchildren, and the many circumstances that affect their lives, like jobs, child support, and court proceedings. Then they can drop their children notes or call to let them know of their prayers and to share relevant passages of Scripture.

Emotional Encouragement

All of the above kinds of encouragement—verbal, material, tangible, and spiritual—also provide emotional encouragement. Encouragement is a gift. It's an "I'm-with-you" frame of mind that bolsters a hurting person's confidence, over and above the encourager's ability to say or do anything extraordinary. Emotional encouragement expresses itself in good listening: positive eye contact, a smile, a gentle touch on the arm or a hug. A good listener gives full attention to the speaker and does not interrupt, correct, or "preach" to the one pouring out the pain and confusion of his heart. In many ways, emotional encouragement is the most important kind, for it creates a safe environment for reciprocal communication that is honest and self-disclosuring. This empowers the hurting one to strengthen *himself*.

BOUNDARIES REVISITED

Encouragement is not required of parents, but your encouragement is always a gift, given with no strings attached. Encouragement must be given with the balance of love and boundaries described in Chapter 7. Encouragement that depletes the encourager is unbalanced and unhealthy. Encouragement must be dispensed according to your resources, never beyond them, and never grudgingly. How and when you express encouragement to your son or daughter, your grandchildren, and to other people affected by the divorce, will depend on three things.

Emotional Resources

Your ability to give encouragement depends on the depth of your own emotional well. It's hard to give encouragement when you feel discouraged yourself! It's also hard to give encouragement while grieving. While experiencing your own pain, you may be able to encourage in some ways but not in others. For example, you may be able to fix a meal for your son or daughter, but not yet emotionally up to baby-sitting for your grandchildren. You may be able to express your love through a greeting card, but not yet able to engage in heart-to-heart conversation. Your emotional resources will ebb and flow with the situation, and they will increase over time. Perhaps the best approach is just to do what you can, when you can.

Material Resources

Not all parents have money to loan or to give. Not all parents have a spare bedroom or an extra car to loan. Not all parents are physically able to baby-sit or handy enough to do home repairs. Even when resources abound, time may be very limited. And even when time and money and energy are abundant, there may be important reasons *not* to share these resources with your child. For example, if your son or daughter would take cash designated for groceries and use it for drugs instead, you would be prudent to make monetary help contingent on your child's getting into treatment. But under normal circumstances, if you have resources to share, great! If you don't, trust that God will meet your child's material needs in ways that do not involve you. You can focus on dispensing other kinds of encouragement.

Emotional and Geographic Proximity

Providing encouragement is difficult when there is distance between the encourager and the one in need, whether the distance be emotional or geographic. Sometimes the crisis brings parent and child back together emotionally and/or geographically, but not always.

When the lines of communication are already weak, the weight of separation and divorce may only stretch them to the breaking point. Marcy said, "I wish that I had had a closer relationship with my parents prior to the separation and divorce so that I could have talked with them before things went totally bad." Joan, whose son was going through a divorce, said, "I just pray and keep my mouth shut, because my son takes things as criticism that are meant as support."

Emotional support can be far more valuable than the physical proximity of parent and child. In fact, sometimes being geographically distant can actually be a plus. Polly, whose parents live ten hours away from her, explains.

> Even though it hurt them not to be with me all the time, I feel that my parents gave me a lot of room to work through this alone. They felt I was well taken care of with all the friends I had ministering to me. After the divorce they told me they finally realized that if they had been with me that I would not have grieved and worked through my emotions because they would have tried to keep the pain away by sheltering me. I grew so much learning to do things for myself and seeking out people to help me. I know my parents would have tried to do everything for me and that would have been so detrimental. I talked to them about this and made them see that they had been right in not being here so much.

LINES OF SUPPORT

A survey of divorcing adults and the parents of divorcing adult children asked them to describe the lines of support and encouragement between the generations. Here are the questions and a sample of the responses.

(To parents of a divorced child): What specific things have you done to support your son or daughter?

Betty: Prayed for him always. Been available when he needed to talk. Helped financially when we could. Bought school clothes for the girls. All of our family has supported him with their love and concern.

Paul: Made ourselves available, encouraged visits, encouraged our son's brothers and sisters to help support and provide emotional support for their brother, pray all the time.

Alice: Occasional cards and encouragements, and after first explaining our attitude, we have withdrawn from engaging in unpleasant subjects. We try to let our daughter set the agenda, but make sure she knows we have no feelings of rejection.

(To divorcing adults): What have your parents done to help you?

Marcy: Encouraged me that the Lord will take care of me.

Polly: They call once a week and come and visit more often, to help me with the house and just to provide love and support. They have offered support financially if I need it. They have paid my way home a couple of times since they live so far away.

Karyn: They were supportive, allowing me to take care of things without interfering. Financially, they helped me buy a car.

(To divorcing adults): What do you wish your parents had done differently with you?

Mike: I wish they had listened. I wish they had been less vindictive toward my wife and more forgiving.

Kelly: I wish they had shown compassion and understanding. A little financial assistance would have been nice. My mother suggested that I go on welfare when I was having financial difficulties early on, with an infant to care for. When we divorced, their attitude was one of relief that I left a man of a different race (a tremendous source of embarrassment for them) and smug satisfaction that I got what I deserved.

John (temporarily lived with his parents while separated from his wife): I think it might have been nice if they had offered to invite my wife over. They knew that I very much wanted to heal the marriage. If they had offered to, I don't know if she would have come, but the offer would have encouraged me.

PROVIDING EMOTIONAL SUPPORT

These comments, both positive and negative, from adult children and their parents, can be helpful to you as you think about ways to encourage your own son or daughter at this time. A year from now, what would you like your child to be saying about the kind of support she received from you during this time?

Parents of divorcing adult children have a tremendous opportunity to touch their children's lives with love and grace. But it's not an easy task!

Your own feelings about the divorce are a mosaic of many things and make it difficult to act decisively or unselfishly.

What are your long-standing beliefs about divorce being "right" or "wrong" in general? In the case at hand? What is the likelihood of reconciliation? What you believe the Bible teaches, what your friends and family believe about divorce, whether you yourself have experienced divorce, and how desperate you believe your child's marital circumstances are—all these beliefs factor into your feelings about divorce. You may discover some cognitive dissonance—a gap—between what you think *ought to be* and what presently *is*. The struggle in your own mind to close the gap can prevent you from supporting and encouraging your child according to their needs.

Remember also that you are in the midst of a grieving process. Your own feelings of shock, anger, and depression will certainly affect your ability to support and encourage others at this time. Outside factors over which you have no control—money problems, grandchildren, the other set of parents, "the other man/woman," addiction, abuse—also complicate the kind and amount of emotional support you can offer.

No matter what your specific combination of circumstances happens to be, divorce is always tough—on you, as well as on your children and grandchildren. In order to support them, you need to stay in touch with what *you* think, what *you* feel, and what *you* need every step of the way. When your tank is full (so to speak) emotionally, spiritually and physically, you are in a better position to give to your loved ones, and to do so creatively with your whole heart.

9

When Your Child Begins to Date Again

I think the first time he brought a girl home to meet us was extremely difficult for all of us—the realization that he's going on, he's got his divorce, and now he's dating again.

—Father of divorced son

Eventually, both parties in the divorce will start to date again—and this will probably happen before you're ready for it. This idea may be very foreign to you. In your generation people were more loyal, more reserved in their relationships. They made many personal sacrifices for their spouses, their families, and for appearances' sake. In other words, they would never date while separated from their spouse, and then they would continue to be very discreet after the divorce was final.

Like it or not, this is a different day and age. You will most likely have to deal with the emotional trauma of seeing your adult child date soon after divorce, if not before. The stereotypical situation is that the man in the marriage is already involved with someone else before any papers are signed, perhaps even before the couple separates. But today, an increasing number of women, as well, are abandoning their marriages in the same way. People seem to move into new relationships without batting an eye.

97

COMMON PARENTAL CONCERNS ABOUT DATING

Getting hurt may be the first concern that comes to mind when your adult child announces he is dating again. There will probably be several more fears that flood your mind in rapid succession.

1. *My son or daughter won't find anyone who will want to date them.* This fear is probably not valid, but obviously depends on your son or daughter's age and circumstances. The majority of divorced men and women eventually remarry, but it will, and should take time. Waiting several years is actually quite healthy.

2. *What about promiscuity and AIDS?* This is a very legitimate concern, but one that you have little control over. Your children are adults who will make their own choices. There is probably little that you can say or do at this point to influence their lifestyle, but that doesn't mean you shouldn't try.

3. *What if we don't like the person our child is dating?* Why don't you wait and give him a chance? If this person seems all wrong for your son or daughter you can try to give non-intrusive guidance. But in the meantime, give your child some credit and see what happens.

4. *How many times will I have to go through this?* Many parents express concern about their child bringing home numerous dates. They wonder how she will adjust if her heart is shattered repeatedly. In reality, it is very unlikely that your child will bring home every date. So relax, and remember, a date is just a date. Enjoy the company and don't get serious or attached to any of their dates until you are told, "This one is serious."

5. *How do I introduce my adult child's dates to friends?* This may be more of a stumbling block than you realize. Ask your

son or daughter how they would like you to handle this. It is usually safe to say, "This is my daughter's friend, Tony." Many adults feel funny about having someone introduce them as "my daughter's boyfriend."

TWO EXTREMES

People have two basic responses to the breakup of their marriages. Some say, "I'll never trust another man (or woman) again" and swear off the opposite sex. Now, the ones who say this don't always mean it, and may be headed for a great fall, but many are very sincere in this vow. Don't be worried if this is your son or daughter's response. In fact, thank God for it. While this attitude might sound bitter, the result is very positive. The reaction will pass, but in the interim your son or daughter will be protected from being hurt again. Completing the grieving cycle may take several years, but this is healthy. Our society is too obsessed with quick fixes. We like fast food and instant results. But healing properly requires time.

Chapter 3 noted that one of the ways parents bargain is to set their newly divorced child up with dates. Never rush your adult child into a new relationship. Resist the temptation to manipulate the situation by playing matchmaker. Similarly, don't encourage him to get back "in action" in order to get over so-and-so. You may mean well, but you will be circumventing the healing process.

A second reaction to the breakup of a marriage is much more dangerous. The individual exclaims, "Free at last; free at last! Oh, thank goodness, I'm free at last!" She can't wait to hit the singles scene and find a new love to meet her needs.

Such a reaction is very natural, but it is not healthy. No

broken person is ever healed by finding someone else to complete his life. A broken person is only healed by allowing time to restore the heart.

From this point on in the chapter, think of yourself as eavesdropping on a counseling session with a divorcing person. What follows is advice that comes from personal experience and years of counseling with hundreds of people.

DATING ADVICE FOR THE SINGLE-AGAIN

As a parent, you can do much to communicate the following principles.

Risks and Cautions

After a divorce most people are seeking emotional affirmation and wholeness. Emotional wholeness comes to those who learn how to balance proper risks with proper cautions. Many take foolish risks (like rebound romances) or observe needless cautions (like hiding away for years). But by keeping the two instincts in balance, the individual can edge his way back to wholeness.

The first risk that a newly divorced person may have to take is to seek help. Maybe that starts with a helpful book. It may involve going to a divorce recovery seminar or seeing a counselor.

The proper caution to balance this risk is to go slowly. Don't expect to make your reentry to normal life overnight. This will be frustrating, but be patient. It takes usually three to five years to learn to trust people again and fully reenter society.

Watch Out for Rebound Relationships

It is not unusual, several months into a relationship, for one partner to ask, "Where is this relationship going?"

The relationship may be great, the interaction comfortable; lots of needs on both ends are being met. The response from the other partner is, "Hey, why ruin a good thing? I'm having a good time, you're having a good time. Let's not ruin it by getting serious."

After several more months, there is another exchange: "Look, if you can't tell me where we're going, I don't know that I can continue this relationship."

Response: "Hey, I don't need that kind of pressure. If you can't just enjoy the relationship, then I'm outta here."

What has happened? Even though it may be years after the divorce, the person has not healed. When he tries to use his heart again, he discovers it still doesn't work right. And both partners get hurt.

For a while the divorced person finds that he's attracted to anybody who strokes his damaged areas. And there are lots of damaged areas. He probably feels rejected, and it is glorious to be wanted and accepted by someone. She may feel rejected sexually, afraid that she's too ugly or not sexy enough. And when someone comes by who finds her sexy, that seems to be just what the doctor ordered. For the moment, it may be satisfying. The danger is that the damaged area gets too much attention, and the relationship is tilted unhealthily in the wrong direction.

Friendships

The most basic emotional needs are not romance and sexual fulfillment, as the talk shows keep telling us, but security and significance. We need relationships in which we know we are accepted. That's security. And we need to give to others whose lives we can touch. That's significance. The divorced person needs to take the risk of finding true friends; yet he or she also needs to avoid "rebound romances."

That's a risk! Newly divorced hearts are still vulnerable. It's not easy for them to open up to others, to let others care for them, and to care for others in return. There's a lot of hurt and a lot of fear.

Solid friendships are the most important boost toward wholeness, but the newly divorced person needs to avoid romance. He may not like to hear it from a parent or anyone else, but romance is fraught with pitfalls for one recovering from divorce. Romance is tempting because it promises to massage wounded areas, but it will probably wound the divorcee all over again.

You know the syndrome: Your self-image is at an all-time low. When someone starts to pay attention to you, it's hard to keep it in perspective. Before you've even spoken with her yet, in your mind's eye you're marching down the aisle together.

A solid, honest, *nonromantic* friendship can allow the adult child to learn who he is, how he acts, and what he has to give in a safe context. So long as your son or daughter *needs* to be remarried, she's not ready for remarriage. When he knows that he's able to live a full, healthy life on his own, only then will he be able to enter a marriage as a giver and a taker.

Discover and Develop Personal Strengths

Often those who have been divorced begin to think of themselves as losers. They wear "defeat-colored glasses." They see their entire lives in terms of their own weaknesses. They only know what they've done wrong. They only see uncertainty and confusion.

In rebuilding their lives, they need to take a good look at

their strengths. As a parent, you can open your child's eyes to what she *can* do. You probably know her better than just about anyone else does. Therefore, you can do much to help them come to grips with their own strengths.

Ask your son or daughter, "What kind of person do you now want to be? Accept where you are: You're divorced. You didn't want to be, but you are. You're hurting. You didn't want to be, but you are. Close your eyes to all that and look forward. *From this point on*, what do you want to become?"

Help Your Child Identify His Assets

As the adult child looks at what he would like to become, help him figure out what his assets already are. Family and friends can be the most helpful with this. They often present an unbiased opinion. Your child may not even realize that she is uncommonly caring, or especially energetic, or good at organizing. She needs family and friends at this difficult time to remind her of her strengths.

Help Your Child Find the Right Kind of People to Hang Out With

Once the adult child has identified his strengths, he needs to find people with similar interests and abilities and begin to associate with them. Encourage him to seek out and become a part of the lives of such people.

For instance, if she wants to be like the people she sees at church, encourage her to go to worship services and fellowship activities. If she admires the people who build houses for the poor with Habitat for Humanity, then she should be encouraged to join that group. If he is interested in acting, suggest he get involved with a community theater. If he likes organizing, encourage him to volunteer his services to a community organization. And if she needs to learn new skills or a new trade to implement her interests, encourage her to attend night school or sign up for a technical or trade program.

Not only will your child enjoy himself and learn new skills: he will also meet others with similar interests and abilities. These may become the basis for new, "safe" friendships. Hopefully your son or daughter will not have to learn the hard way that the bars and most singles' clubs have nothing to offer for building up interests or establishing meaningful relationships.

Learn to Love Others Again

One of the last things that the divorced person is able to do is to trust, commit, and truly love others again. As a parent, you can help them immensely in this area by demonstrating unconditional love and support for her. You may be the only significant relationship in her life which has not been betrayed. If she is to learn to love others again, she will need your example.

This kind of love goes beyond developing a healthy self-image and establishing supportive new friendships. Unconditional love is experienced only through a relationship with God, and at times with our most precious loved ones.

After what your son or daughter has been through, it is understandable that he or she will have a hard time in a trusting, committed relationship. So if you find her cringing at the mere thought of growing emotionally close to others, be aware that it's all part of the self-protection that is so necessary for a while. If she allows God to heal her life, if he turns to Him as the source of strength and love, this will most likely pass. While your child will probably stumble many times during the divorce recovery process, with your prayers, support, and example, he can overcome his fears and learn to love and trust others again.

PART III

Grandparenting After Divorce

10

Divorce and Your Grandchildren: The Effects

Divorce is when your mom and dad get separated and live in different places. This happens when they stop loving each other. Divorce hurts. My stomach hurts because I kept my feelings inside. . . . I felt like I was being pulled apart.[1]
—*Stephen, age 8*

Cindy's parents divorced when she was seventeen years old. Eight years later, as a twenty-five-year-old woman, Cindy sought counseling to find out why she had such poor luck in relationships, particularly with men. In just two years, Cindy had broken off four serious relationships.

For Cindy, the pattern was always the same. She would grow closer and closer to a man, emotionally, until the time when some type of commitment was implied. Then the difficulties would start. Cindy would usually set up some type of trap in which she tested the character of her beau. Sometimes she would check and recheck his whereabouts, even though he would tell her ahead of time where he would be. Other times she demanded that he account for every moment of his time when asked, "What did you do today?"

---

1. Gary Sprague, *My Parents Got a Divorce: Kids Tell How They Went from Hurt to Hope* (Elgin, Illinois: David C. Cook Publishing), 85.

On one occasion Cindy became incensed by her boyfriend's "dishonesty": He failed to mention that he had called for her earlier in the evening and talked briefly with her roommate. From that point on, Cindy became suspicious that there was something going on between her boyfriend and her roommate. Needless to say, the romantic relationship did not last much longer, and Cindy's relationship with her roommate grew extremely strained.

Cindy's difficulties lay in the fact that her childhood memories were interfering with her life in the present. Cindy had first learned of her father's "indiscretions" when she was about ten, and she had many memories of heated arguments between her parents over suspected affairs. After her parents finally divorced, Cindy's mother and grandparents made a point of continually reminding her about how devious her father had been. Now, like many other young women with her background, Cindy has difficulty with commitment and trust. She is an example of a young woman struggling with the long-term effects of parental divorce.

CHILDREN AND DIVORCE

Each year (since 1972), more than one million children see their parents divorce. This means that every year roughly two percent of the total child population experiences the trauma of divorce. The cumulative result is that today two out of every five children in our nation are children of divorce.

One well-known researcher, Judith Wallerstein, followed children of divorce for over twenty years to trace the effects of divorce on their lives. Her books, along with many follow-up articles and books, have given adult children of divorce the courage to come forward in order to tell their stories. Their attitude: "I'm glad someone is finally recognizing and documenting the dramatic impact of divorce on families."

SHORT-TERM EFFECTS

The short-term effects of divorce are those reactions which begin immediately and can last for several years. Your grandchildren will go through stages of grieving similar to those experienced by adults, as discussed in Chapters 2, 3, and 4. It is likely that they will become depressed and lethargic, or anxious and more active. You may observe them regressing at home and in their schoolwork. Boys may become more aggressive, and girls more defiant. Teens will sometimes demonstrate increased rebellion.

In general, all children feel fear, anger, rejection, and loneliness in the wake of divorce. But children respond differently to divorce according to their ages. This is because divorce enters their lives at different developmental stages.

Preschoolers

Toddlers and preschoolers understand the least about what is going on in a divorce and often demonstrate the most dramatic reactions. Fearful and bewildered, they may regress in their behavior, have trouble sleeping, or experience heightened anxiety when separated from the parent to whom they are most attached. They may be clingy, needy, or prone to outbursts of temper. They are the age group most likely to blame themselves for their parents' divorce.

Early School-Age

Children whose parents divorce when they are five to eight years old typically experience intense sadness. Boys especially yearn for absent fathers, and they find it difficult even to be angry with their dads. This age group is also very sensitive to the material losses of divorce and fears deprivation. These children may fantasize about their mom and dad getting back together.

Pre-Adolescents

Older children, ages nine to twelve, often become angry about divorce. They may feel embarrassed and upset with their parents for "breaking the rules" and may cope with their feelings by staying busy. When there is a great deal of hostility between parents, these children may take sides with one parent, viewing things in terms of black and white and designating one parent as the "good guy" and the other as the "bad guy." This age group is also prone to somatic complaints—headaches, stomachaches, etc.

Teens

Teenagers are processing the loss of their childhood along with the losses of divorce and may deal with their stress by creating a temporary emotional distance between themselves and their parents. They worry about sex and marriage, and many take a dim view of their own ability to succeed in these areas because of their parents' failures. Some teens act out their distress by using alcohol or drugs or becoming sexually active. But for others, the divorce of their parents acts as a tutor, stimulating moral and spiritual growth, a more realistic view of money, and responsible behavior and decisions.

The short-term reactions will end when your grandchildren reach the point of accepting the new family system and structure. A remarriage or any major change during the grieving process can significantly delay their recovery. Often, major changes like moving to a more affordable house or taking a new job are unavoidable. But for the sake of the children, major changes are best made as slowly and undramatically as possible.

LONG-TERM EFFECTS

Short-term reactions do not necessarily predict how a child will fare in the long run. Many things influence children through the years as they grow up. After your grandchildren have worked through the grieving of their family breakup, they will still have to work through the implications of growing up in a divorced home. These long-term effects may last up to twenty years for some adult children of divorce, and may be permanent.

Recovery from divorce can be measured psychologically in terms of healthy coping skills, degree of depression or anxiety, decisiveness, success in personal relationships, and productivity. Using these as a scale, children of divorce fall into three groups of roughly equal size. Approximately one third of the children of divorce recover very well. Another third recover moderately well. A final third never seem to fully recover from the trauma of their parents' divorce.

The majority who cope fairly well and are able move on

with their lives seem quite normal to those around them. Outwardly they lead healthy, productive lives. Yet even for these people, divorce plays a dramatic role in shaping personality, character, interests, and ambitions.

Children who cope very well with divorce have certain factors in common, as do children who cope very poorly. By knowing what fosters good adjustment and what hinders it, parents and grandparents can strive together to give their children the best shot at a good recovery.

The Age of the Child

It is now known that many of the children who cope best with divorce in the long run are those who were very young when their parents' marriage broke up. Judith Wallerstein's research with children ten years after divorce showed that 68 percent of those who had been preschoolers at the time of the divorce were doing well, compared with less than 40 percent of the older children. This may be due to the fact that younger children are often more shielded from family conflict than older children. In addition, because preschoolers still need so much physical care, they may receive more attention than older children during a family crisis like divorce.

In general, the less time a child spends in a conflicted or dysfunctional environment, the better. Often, the younger the child, the less exposure he will have had to serious situations like abuse or addiction. He will also grow up with less of a "before divorce" and "after divorce" comparison than older children, and fewer painful conscious memories.

The Number of Changes

The impact of divorce upon children is greater when they are exposed to other life stresses. All of these changes add stress:

- moving to a new home
- attending a new church
- moving to a new school district
- adding a new spouse to the family
- having to give up a pet
- an at-home mom going to work full-time
- blending a family.

Wherever possible, try to encourage your adult child to limit the number of changes she makes in the family's life, or at least to make them as slowly as possible. Help her to make wise decisions if you can, and perhaps even make sacrifices in order to help her provide stability for the children.

The Adjustment of the Custodial Parent

While both parents are of key importance in the eventual well-being of the children, the emotional health of the custodial parent (usually Mom) is the greatest predictor of the children's adjustment. Therefore, it is important for you to support the custodial parent if at all possible. Whether this is your daughter or your daughter-in-law, don't participate in any "punishment" of her or contribute in any way to the misery of the situation. Try not to belittle or badmouth either parent in front of the grandchildren.

Almost all couples have severe conflicts during the early

stages of marital breakup, but if these continue well beyond the divorce, they can suck all participants back into the black hole of conflict for more years than is necessary. If people continue "throwing rocks in the water," the ripples of divorce will continue to affect the lives of your grandchildren, your children, and you. For everyone's sake, let the waters calm.

Since children spend the majority of their time with the custodial parent, it stands to reason that the custodial parent's attitudes will influence the children. If you antagonize the custodial parent, it is very likely that you will hurt your own relationship with your grandchildren. Right or wrong, like it or not, these are the facts of post-divorce life. Choose an attitude of forgiveness and reconciliation. In so doing, you will be a wonderful role model for your children and your grandchildren.

The Relationship with the Noncustodial Parent

For years the importance of the relationship with the noncustodial parent (usually Dad) has been ignored. Within the past five years or so, the noncustodial parent has emerged as a key player. A primary reason for negative effects of divorce on children is the loss of contact with the father. Consistent and frequent contact with the noncustodial parent correlates with well-adjusted children, unless the father is abusive or otherwise unfit. The relationship with father is linked to identity with the opposite sex for girls, ambition and motivation for boys, and overall adjustment and relating abilities for both sexes. Therefore, it is critically important that you also encourage your grandchildren to love and respect their father, in spite of any wrongs he may have committed.

One father described his son-in-law as a louse. Wine,

women, money—you name it, this guy had abused it. When it was suggested he not share these thoughts with his grandchildren, he was surprised.

"They need to know the truth about their father," he protested.

But he followed the advice, and vented his displeasure only to his wife or at times to his daughter. In time he was able to see that his son-in-law, while being a poor husband, was really a very good father. He was very consistent and responsible with his visits and was greatly loved by his children. Holding on to their belief and respect for their father turned out to be a critical element in the children's emotional well-being.

Key Point: Don't rob your grandchildren of their ability to love both their parents.

Other Traumas

Most of the children who never seem to recover from their parents' divorce are the ones who also have to contend with other specific traumas. These traumas include (but are not limited to) physical abuse, sexual abuse, severe emotional or verbal abuse, extended neglect, drug or alcohol addiction of one or both parents, and mental illness in the family. For children exposed to one or more of these preexisting conditions, the long-term implications of divorce are more serious. This does not imply that if your grandchild was exposed to one or more of these traumas, he will be irreparably harmed. The presence of such factors merely indicates a greater propensity for long-term problems, and therefore you need to be particularly sensitive to your grandchildren's needs and emotional condition.

When any of these complicating factors are present, you

need to assess how much you can do to help the family. Does there need to be a family intervention? How strongly do you need to voice your opinions? How much can you help the grandchildren while your own child puts his life in order?

There are no easy answers. However, be sure you do not condone or cover for any kind of abuse. Intervene or notify authorities, but don't keep silent when little ones are at risk.

CASE STUDIES

As you seek to assist your grandchildren in their recovery from divorce, there are attitudes and behavior to watch for. The following case studies are typical. These scenarios are true, but the names and some of the details have been altered in order to protect the identities of the children.

Jason: Diminished Motivation

Jason first came to see me when he was fifteen. He wore long hair, torn jeans, a punk rock T-shirt, and a sour look on his face. Jason was actually referred by his mom because he had decided to drop out of school. Mom said she would permit it if he would go to three counseling sessions.

Every topic brought up for conversation was met with silence or an occasional "yep" or "nope." Finally, as a last resort, I decided to bring up a subject *he* was interested in: punk rock and heavy metal music.

Suddenly Jason became very animated and talkative. He was surprised that I had shown any interest. He later stated that no other adult had ever shown interest in this topic, which he valued so highly. Adults usually walked away or told him to turn it off. Jason talked about all the groups, the most popular songs, and the meaning behind the lyrics. He then of-fered to bring his tape player next week, along with a couple of his favorite tapes.

To make a long story short, Jason continued coming, by choice, for the next six months. During that time, he began to tell about his family, his life, and his feelings. Jason was a very angry young man. His father had left the home when he was about nine years old and moved in with another woman. The new woman had children of her own and was soon pregnant again. As his dad gradually broke off contact with his former family, Jason felt more rejection, resentment, and anger. He withdrew emotionally and isolated himself in his room with his music and an occasional cigarette.

Jason's mother and grandparents were quite frustrated with the situation, yet Jason seemed to have more respect for his grandfather than any other adult. We were able to use this rela-tionship as a way to build positive interactions between Jason and this stable male role model. The grandfather's role was to provide a listening ear, give Jason a sense of unconditional love, and to offer supportive advice.

Jason's main problem was his attitude and motivation. He had given up on life by the time he was fourteen. After all, life wasn't fair. He couldn't even sustain his father's love.

Even though Jason was intelligent and talented, he had a difficult time finding direction or purpose in life. He felt he had no control over his own life.

This young man's problem is a common one. The sense of being unable to control one's own life appears in approximately 45 percent of the male children of divorce. Dropping out of school, not attending college or else bumbling their way through college, and being underemployed after school, are all indicators of this phenomenon.

There is mounting evidence that boys who do not have a positive male role model, either a father or grandfather, have increased difficulty in maintaining commitments. Observing men in committed relationships seems to have a positive effect on children. Those who miss this opportunity seem to be affected negatively.

Today, Jason works in a factory. He finished high school, but went no further in schooling even though he has above average intelligence. He is socially active and appears to be much happier today. His hair is still long, but his taste in music has moderated. To his friends, he's an average twenty-four-year-old and a nice guy. But to me he is a struggling soul. With the help of his extended family and friends, Jason can work through his issues and lead a productive life. Yes, he will struggle with commitment, and yes, he will battle underachievement, but with support and proper choices he doesn't have to remain a victim.

Latishia: The Sleeper Effect

Latishia is a twenty-six-year-old adult child of divorce. Her parents split up when she was just three, and she gradually lost all contact with her father over a period of two years. Her mother struggled with drug and alcohol problems throughout Latishia's early years, and there were many times in Latishia's life when her mother was incapable of caring for her. During those times she lived with her grandmother. Latishia's grandmother was also divorced so there was no male role model in either home.

Just before she turned ten, Latishia finally went to live with her mother. But she remained very close to her grandmother: They continued to attend church together since Mom chose not to go, and Latishia stayed with her grandmother regularly due to Mom's extended work schedule.

For a long time. Latishia appeared to come through her mother's divorce and her unstable living situation better than one might expect. But during adolescence (as is often the case), Latishia began to have difficulties. She resented her mother and judged her for not being available in her early years. Perhaps it wasn't until then that she began to understand the implications of her father's abandonment and her mother's addictions.

Latishia found her first "true love" when she was sixteen. She became attached to him very quickly and was devastated when he eventually broke up with her. After that experience, Latishia had little to do with guys.

Now Latishia is active in her church singles' group. She has a strong belief in a heavenly Father who loves her unconditionally and in whom she finds her acceptance. Yet this does not seem to carry over into her relationships with men. She openly talks about her mistrust of men, and she feels discomfort whenever she is around any man who is her age or older. She says that she would like to be married someday, but that any prospects would have to be in the distant future. She knows that she is very picky when it comes to men and that is why she still does not date very much.

Latishia's delayed reaction to her parents' divorce is known as the sleeper effect and has been documented in approximately 66 percent of the female children of divorce. The sleeper effect occurs quite often in women who previously seemed to be handling their parents' divorce fairly well. The negative effects of divorce suddenly emerge during the teenage years or during the early twenties, a critical time in life when women are making important decisions about dating, marriage, career, and higher education.

A common element in the sleeper effect is fear: fear of commitment and fear of betrayal. For some, the fear may lead to the coping strategy of control. In other words, "If I can learn how to control men or control the situation, then I won't be hurt again."

Another coping strategy seen in both women and men is avoidance. This can include avoidance of significant relating or any kind of commitment. Usually, patterns of relating are developed in which relationships reach a certain level and then "self destruct." This can include an inability to communicate deeper than on a superficial level, an inability to make a commitment, or an inability to allow the relationship to grow beyond a friendship or a purely sexual basis.

The combination of control and avoidance can reach extreme levels among some adult children of divorce. This is evidenced by a disproportionately high number of both men and women who are promiscuous, homosexual, in treatment facilities for personality disorders, or divorced themselves. Without the realization of these destructive patterns of relating, these difficulties may follow them the rest of their lives.

Kathy: The Overburdened Child

The first time I met Kathy, I was amazed at what a responsible, mature child she was at age fourteen. Her mother was quite proud of the fact that teachers and friends alike commented on what a good job she had done in raising her daughter all alone. The presenting problem was that they were having difficulty in choosing a college. (Most kids are not even thinking about college at age fourteen.) Kathy wanted to go away for school; her mother, on the other hand, wanted Kathy to stay home so that she could continue to provide the proper guidance to her daughter.

Since college was still three years away and Kathy was so responsible, it was odd that this was such a burning issue. But soon it became evident that the reason Mom needed Kathy to stay home was to help Mother "keep it together." Kathy was the one who kept the house in order. She took care of her younger siblings before and after school, prepared the evening meal, and asked Mom all about her day when she got home from work. Kathy did not go out socially during the week or on weekends because she was needed at home. If Mom did happen to go out on a date, which was rarely, she always solicited Kathy's opinion of her suitor because, as she stated, "Kathy's a better judge of character than I am."

Today Kathy is eighteen and a prime example of the overburdened child. She ended up attending the local community college and living at home because she feels she is needed there.

When a marriage breaks down it is common for both the mother and the father to do less parenting. The custodial parent (usually the mother) is worn down by the changes in her life, possibly including a move to a different house or apartment, job changes, new financial responsibilities, and parenting alone. The estranged parent (usually the father) feels guilty because he is not there for the kids as often as he'd like to be and just wants their times together to be enjoyable. Therefore, both parents tend to discipline less, spend less time with their children, and may be less sensitive to their needs.

Unable to meet the challenges of parenting as a single, many parents begin to lean on their children to pick up the slack. Their children become latchkey kids, home in an empty house, assuming major responsibilities long before they may actually be ready to handle them. An overburdened child's role may include keeping house, baby-sitting younger siblings, acting as the "man of the house," mediating arguments, serving as the parent's confidant, and emotionally supporting the parent. While most of these roles are not intentionally conferred upon the child, the child's role becomes integral to the well-being of the parent or the family. The divorce itself may not be the cause but does serve as a catalyst for bringing to the surface specific emotional difficulties.

When a child takes on so much responsibility so early in life, there are consequences later on. Either the child rebels and becomes overly irresponsible or he continues in the overburdened lifestyle and suffers perfectionism, a nervous breakdown, overly nurturing relationships, over-parenting, or losing personal identity for a cause or another person.

As a grandparent, you can be aware of the potential risk of an overburdened child and keep an eye on your own grandchildren. Everyone in a divorcing family will have increased responsibilities, but the critical issue is whether or not the children are taking on more than they should have to and if the parent-child roles are being reversed. This is where grandparents can play such a critical role in the well-being of the grandchildren. Many times they can fill in the parenting gap temporarily while the parents work on rebuilding their lives.

A Challenge for Grandparents

Divorce never stands alone as a onetime traumatic event but is experienced as an ongoing struggle. It begins with an unhappy marriage, progresses through custody battles and court hearings, and continues with ripple effects that may continue for generations.

However, when the parents and grandparents make decisions including what's best for the children, chances for long-term positive effects increase. Positive effects of divorce can include:

- Greater sensitivity to others and their problems
- Increased responsibility and greater maturity
- A more realistic outlook on life, especially on life's disappointments and pain
- Increased motivation to succeed at one's own marriage.

As grandparents, your stability and support may mean the difference between passing the ills of divorce on to the next generation or softening the impact of divorce on everyone concerned. God is able to use you as agents of grace and healing in the lives of your children and grandchildren.

11

How to Help
Your Grandchildren Cope

Life's disappointments are veiled love's appointments.
—Rev. C. A. Fox

Child psychologists believe that parental divorce ranks second only to parental death in severity of childhood traumas. Indeed, to children divorce is an emotional earthquake of mammoth proportions that uproots all of life, entirely against their wishes. It is an unparalleled crisis in their young lives. Divorce is not only uniquely painful, it is uniquely ironic: in divorce, the very people children count on for comfort and security, become the *source* of their profound discomfort and insecurity. And as children's needs for reassurance are escalating in the face of divorce, parents in pain are less sensitive to their children and less capable of meeting their needs.

Typically, it takes three to five years for parents and children to regain their equilibrium after a divorce; to adjust and settle into a post-divorce lifestyle. During those years, both the custodial and noncustodial parent are reeling emotionally from the shock waves, and making all sorts of major decisions about housing, employment, remarriage, and finances. They are frequently overwhelmed and depressed (particularly single mothers). Both financial and emotional resources can be stretched to the breaking point. It should come as no surprise, then, that the quality of parenting children experience in the wake of divorce is usually diminished.

During these critical years, and beyond, grandparents can make a tremendous contribution to the lives of their grandchildren. The support and encouragement of grandparents can remind children that they have roots, that they "belong," and that the rest of their family is stable. Most important, by providing consistent nurture and comfort, grandparents can become an emotional "safe place" that gives children a sense of love and security.

John describes the safe place his parents provided for their grandchildren.

> I was alone for a long time before I remarried. So there were a lot of years when I would go to my parents' home and I would bring the children. Grandma and Grandpa's house more or less became the place of stability in the family. To this day they are still in that house, so that's probably the most stable single location in my children's memory. They have really been a wonderful blessing in many ways. They are the gathering place now. My kids love to go to their home.

Not all grandparents want to be as involved in the lives of their grandchildren as John's parents are. In Judith Wallerstein's *Second Chances*, one study of sixty families in the process of divorce, only half of the maternal grandparents and less than half of the paternal grandparents stayed in touch with their grandchildren. Assuming, however, that your grandchildren will be among those whose grandparents make the effort to maintain contact, the following suggestions may be helpful.

WAYS TO HELP YOUR GRANDCHILDREN

There are many, many practical ways to provide help and encouragement to your grandchildren. What you can do will depend on

- how close you live to them
- the kind of relationship you presently enjoy with them and their parent(s)
- your motivation, energy, creativity, and resources.

Every grandparent-grandchild relationship is different. If you presently have a strong relationship with your grandchild, you are in an ideal position to be supportive. If the present relationship is weaker than you would like, determine to build it up with a positive attitude and with prayer. Here are some tips.

Seek a Good Relationship

The first step to fostering a good relationship with your grandchildren is to bolster your relationship with their parents. Divorce can put an extra strain on intergenerational communication, particularly in cases where parent and child may have experienced difficulty relating in the first place. But the relationship between grown children and their parents and/or in-laws is what permits and mediates the connection between grandparents and grandchildren. Author Carolyn Jabs has advised parents, ". . . if your relationship is strained and you want your children to have a rewarding bond with their grandparents, the single most important thing you can do is to get your own relationships with the previous generation in order." She quotes Dr. Joan Aldous, a professor of sociology at Notre Dame: "'. . . if you complain about your mother-in-law or fall silent whenever your father walks into the room, your children are unlikely to form warm relationships with these people.'"[1]

The relationship between you and your grandchildren's parents is important for another reason. The most important factor in a child's recovery from divorce is the emotional health of the parent the child lives with. So, whatever you can do to help and encourage the custodial parent indirectly benefits the child as well.

Accept Your Grandchildren

Peggy's daughter and son-in-law have divorced. Her grandson, Justin, has been rejected by his other set of grandparents. Peggy explained, "They do not accept Justin as a grandchild because he is adopted. They say, 'He is not our grandson.'" Peggy's husband, Jack, added, "They have nothing to do with him. So he has only one set of grandparents—us!"

Kelly's story was more positive. She recounted, "My husband was a black man from East Africa. My parents are openly bigoted. They ordered me to break off with him before our marriage because of his race. Get the picture?" Kelly and her husband separated shortly after their only child was born, and her parents were happy to see the marriage end. This being the case, Kelly has been pleasantly surprised by her parents' acceptance of her biracial son. "My parents seem to accept Daryl and don't treat him differently than their other grandchildren."

---

1. Carolyn Jabs, "Generations," *Sesame Street Magazine Parents' Guide*, November 1988, 24.

Do you have adopted grandchildren? Biracial grandchildren? Handicapped (mentally or physically) grandchildren? If so, how do you feel about them? Does the divorce of their parents change the way you think about them? Special children pose special challenges for grandparents. But the truth is, they need you just as much whether their parents are married or divorced.

Be a Mentor

Many children who recover well from parental divorce have a *mentor*. A mentor is an adult other than Mom or Dad who is involved in the child's life and with whom the child shares an interest. Grandparents can make wonderful mentors!

To be a mentor, there must be a relationship, or the potential for a relationship, between the grandparent and the grandchild that "clicks." In other words, as in all successful human relationships, there must be compatible chemistry between the two individuals. In addition, there must be a common interest. This could be anything: stamp collecting, piano playing, sports, computers, cross-stitch. What does your grandchild enjoy doing that you also enjoy doing? When there is relational chemistry and the two people share a common interest, then a grandparent must choose to involve himself in the child's life in a committed, consistent way.

Mentors are valuable to children because they have a positive effect on their self-esteem. If Mom and Dad are too busy or too stressed to focus their time and emotional energy on a child, a grandparent-mentor helps the child believe that she is worthwhile and special. By concentrating on a special interest together with his mentor, the child comes to understand that his grandparent believes in him and that he has talents and abilities he can feel good about.

Be Careful What You Say

Be very careful that you do not damage your grandchild's image of her mother or father with thoughtless negative comments or criticisms. You have a right to your opinions, of course, and you have a need to express your feelings (as discussed in Chapter 6), but take care never to do this in the child's hearing. Do not allow others to do this either. You can handle inappropriate comments diplomatically by suggesting to the other party that there might be a better time to discuss these things, when there is some privacy.

Be equally careful not to feed false hopes for reconciliation. At certain ages, children are prone to fantasize about Mom and Dad getting back together. Almost always, the chances of this happening are slim. Don't help build your grandchild up for a big disappointment. If his parents do reconcile, everyone will certainly rejoice. But don't encourage false hopes or pray with the child for God to restore the marriage. Doing so could give him a false picture of prayer and contribute to his disappointment with God as well as with his parents. In most cases, it is far kinder to help the child deal with reality. Gently explain that divorce is permanent, and that this means Mom and Dad will not be married to each other any more. Remind the child (when true), that divorce does not change her mom or dad's love for her and that they will always be her parents and take care of her. Patiently listen to her questions and reassure her. In other words, focus on the positive, but be truthful and realistic too.

Be a Good Listener

The greatest compliment you can pay a grandchild is to give that child your full attention when he speaks. By willingly giving your time and concentrating your attention on him, you honor him and confer respect.

All children love adult attention, but children of divorce need it more than most. Unfortunately, they rarely find it during the crisis of parental divorce. In one study, fewer than 10 percent of the children interviewed could recall *any* adult who had even so much as *spoken* sympathetically to them during the breakup of their homes. Adults, naturally, are more comfortable speaking with and commiserating with, other adults. Children often fall through the cracks. But you can make sure this doesn't happen to your grandchildren!

Listening to children can be a chore, but it is also a privilege. If your grandchildren are already comfortable enough to talk with you about their parents and what is going on at home, take the time to listen attentively. If your grandchildren are hesitant to open up, you can nurture their confidence over time. Here are some tips on effective listening.

1. *When a grandchild opens up and begins to share with you, realize that you may be the only adult who has the time and the concern to listen to what he has to say.* Be sure not to argue with him or to contradict his feelings. Avoid telling him what he *should* do or feel. These attitudes are guaranteed to shut down communication. Instead, just accept what he is saying without trying to set him straight. Give him the luxury of being able to share all his feelings honestly with a person who genuinely cares about him.

2. *Sit on the same eye level with the child.* With younger children, this may mean getting down on the floor or pulling the child into your lap. To do so prevents the feeling that you are talking down to them. On the same eye level, you can make positive eye contact with the child as she talks to you.

3. *You can jump-start conversations with children by asking questions.* Avoid *why* questions, however (Why did you make the sky red in this picture? Why are you mad at Bobby?). Nine times out of ten, a child answers a *why* question with "I don't know," and the conversation stalls. A better *what* question is: What did you do in art class today? What did Bobby do to make you so mad? A *what* question is a question a child can answer!

Another good approach is *tell me about.* You can say, "Connie, tell me about this picture you drew," or "Tell me about what happened on the playground with Bobby." This is an invitation to talk, and usually a child will take you up on it.

4. *Use your countenance and your tone of voice to communicate love and acceptance.* When you see your grandchild, let your face light up. Be sure to smile frequently and to speak in a calm voice. If a child senses that you think he is special, he will begin to feel special.

5. *Use touch.* Hugs, pats, "high five," and holding a child's hand can make her feel loved and secure. Younger children love to be held on your lap, rocked, or go for piggyback rides. Jesus often touched the people He ministered to, and He held and touched the children who were brought to him. Touch communicates acceptance, and this helps the child accept himself at a time when he may be feeling rejected or distant from his parents.

6. *With a school-aged child or teenager, three things will help her feel that you are really listening:* First, reflect her own words back to her: Say, "I hear you saying that . . ." (then repeat what she has told you). This lets her know you heard and understood what she said. It also gives her the opportunity to fine-tune the communication or to correct misunderstandings.

Second, pick up on the feelings behind the words. Say,

"Jeff, it sounds like you are feeling pretty disappointed." Jeff can respond by either confirming or denying this, again to help clarify for both of you what's inside.

Third, ask for clarification. Pick up on a word your grandchild uses and seek to expand its meaning: "When you say you are 'down' today, what do you mean exactly?" This lets him know you are paying attention, and that you care enough to really try and understand.

7. *Keep confidences.* If your grandchild trusts you and believes you will keep your conversations with her private, then determine to be worthy of her trust. When there is something you feel you must share with her parent or teacher, first ask permission. Of course, in cases of abuse or other equally serious matters, you must speak out in order to protect the child. But even when this is the case, discuss with your grandchild the reasons you feel you must take this action.

Encourage Your Grandchild to Love Both Parents

No matter what a child's mother or father has done, they are still the only parents a child will ever have. Your grandchild's self-esteem is drawn from her relationship with both Mom and Dad. Never pressure a child to take sides against one parent, and never make statements like "You're better off without him anyway." Children are under a biblical mandate to "honor your father and your mother" (Ex. 20:12). This is the only one of the Ten Commandments that comes with a promise of blessing for obedience: "that your days may be long upon the land which the LORD your God is giving you." Don't stifle your grandchild's affection for both parents!

Give Practical Help

Like adults, kids often need more than kind words and a listening ear. They have many legitimate practical needs every day. But in single-parent families there are often more needs than a parent can humanly, reasonably meet. And the more kids, the more needs that may be "on hold" within the family. Your grandchild may need help with homework or a ride to basketball practice. Your granddaughter may need her bangs trimmed; your grandson may need a patch sewn on his Boy Scout uniform. Have they been to the dentist lately? Do they need new tennis shoes? Does anyone come to watch when they compete in sports or cheerleading? Who goes to parent-teacher conferences?

Single parents sometimes feel defeated because, while they love their kids, they just can't do it all. A grandparent who can step in and lift some of the burden is a blessing to both parent and child. Get into the habit of simply asking yourself, "What does this child need?" If it's a need you can meet—go to it!

Encourage Help and Support from Others

Generally speaking, the more support and encouragement your grandchild receives from others, the better. Peer support is known to be beneficial. Your grandchild may have other friends whose parents are divorced, and the children may already be encouraging and supporting one another. If so, great! Whether this is the case or not, if your grandchild's school offers support and discussion groups for children from divorced homes, encourage your grandchild to participate. These kinds of groups have proven very helpful and encouraging.

Support from other adults is important, too. Your grandchild may benefit from spending time talking with a counselor,

a pastor, his coach, or a scouting leader about the divorce—
about anything or nothing in particular. Most important is that
she feels emotionally nourished and supported by the adults in
her life, outside of the family unit. Encourage positive relationships between your grandchildren and trustworthy adults.

LONG DISTANCE GRANDPARENTING

Like many grandparents today, you may live hundreds or
thousands of miles from your grandchildren. That need not
keep you from offering support and encouragement. All you
need is a determination to stay in touch and a little extra creativity. Here are some ideas.

1. Use your tape recorder to send audio letters. With
younger children, you can borrow books from the library and
read stories to them. You can also sing lullabies or silly songs!

2. Send greeting cards. Children love mail and usually
don't get very much. One major card company has come out
with a line of cards just for adults to send to children. Many of
them focus specifically on building up children of divorce.
Postcards cost less and are just as much fun,

3. Send photographs.

4. Use the photos you receive from your son or daughter to
compose a story about you and your grandchild. Buy a blank
photo album, and type or write some text to insert with each
picture. Simply put the photos in a logical sequence and tell a
story that matches up with the pictures. For example, "Last
Easter Grandma and Grandpa came to visit Cody" (first photo);
"They were the happiest Grandma and Grandpa in the world

when Cody met them at the airport!" *(second photo)*; "Boy! Look at all the good things the Easter Bunny brought Cody!" *(third photo)*. The next time you visit, shoot your photos with this purpose in mind.

5. Telephone on a regular basis, and be sure to speak to each grandchild when you call.

6. If the equipment and expertise is available on both ends, you can fax something to your grandchildren occasionally or communicate via computer modem.

7. Choose a TV show to watch at the same time, then call your grandchild after it is over and discuss it.

8. Bake some chocolate chip cookies or other goody the child loves and send a batch through the mail.

9. Send a Valentine's Day, Easter, April Fool's, or New Year's care package in advance of the holiday. You can include window or door decorations or a homemade party kit—streamers, balloons, paper plates, party hats, and munchies.

10. You can play with your grandchild by sending something silly, like a photocopy of your hand or your face! How about a picture of you doing something childish like making a snow angel, sitting in a tree, or blowing bubbles?

The main point is keeping in touch. How you do it will vary with your personality, your finances, and your playfulness!

What if you want to keep in touch with your grandchildren but one or both of the parents has thrown up a roadblock? What happens when the two generations that had nothing to do with the divorce—grandparents and grandchildren—are kept apart from each other because of the marital dispute? Take heart: Grandparents do have rights, as the next chapter discusses.

12

Grandparents' Rights

> First say to yourself what you would be; then do what you have to do.
> —*Epictetus, c. A.D. 50–120*

One author has noted, ". . . it is an unfortunate fact of modern life that the terrible toll of a skyrocketing divorce rate has so often victimized grandparents and their grandchildren."[1] She is right. Divorce often severs not only the husband-wife relationship, but also the grandparent-grandchild relationship. Sometimes this is because grandparents don't care to keep in touch, but sometimes it is because one or both parents don't want them to keep in touch.

According to Grandparents'–Children's Rights, Inc., the parents who deny grandparents visitation with their children can be divided into three groups of almost equal size.

1. One group consists of intact families (the natural parents and their children). The parents may either be married to

---

1. Eda LaShan, *Grandparenting in a Changing World* (New York: Newmarket Press, 1993), 101.

each other and have never been divorced, or they may be living together but unmarried. Either way, these parents do not allow the grandparents to see their grandchildren.

2. Another group is comprised of parents whose spouse has died. The surviving parent and/or a stepparent will not permit the deceased's parents to visit with their grandchildren. According to one attorney, this happens most often when a father dies and the children are left in the care of their mother.

3. The final group is the group related to divorce. In these cases, either due to divorce, a custody dispute, or a stepparent adoption, the custodial parent and/or the stepparent will deny visitation to the noncustodial parent and grandparents.

In cases when fathers drop out of their children's lives and therefore are not involved in arranging for visits with the paternal grandparents, the mother may not be as motivated to bridge the gap between her children and her former in-laws. However, Grandparents'–Children's Rights, Inc., notes that since 1990 they have received an increase in letters from grandparents who are being denied visitation by their own children.

WHY?

Building memories with grandparents and gaining an understanding and appreciation of one's cultural and biological roots seem to be basic rights of children. Why, then, would parents deny their children access to their grandparents? Why would they stand in the way of a healthy, nurturing relationship with the older generation? Why would they keep children from discovering their heritage and maintaining a normal connection with their extended family? There are many reasons, of course, but in the aftermath of divorce, the issue is often sheer bitterness, vindictiveness, or a desire to "get even." As mentioned in Chapter 8, grandchildren are one of the loyalty issues of divorce.

Sometimes a parent may be dealing with residual issues from childhood; another may be trying to gain a sense of being powerful or in control. In some cases an adult child whose lifestyle is at odds with those of the parents may keep the children away so that he will not have to defend or explain his choices.

No matter what the reasons may be, keep in mind that there is no such thing as an ex-grandparent! Other than parents, grandparents provide the children's most important relationship. Don't allow yourself to be shut out of the lives of your grandchildren, and do whatever you need to do to preserve that relationship.

Many disputes about grandparent visitation can be resolved with a genuine attempt by both parties to communicate and understand. Other times an impasse can be resolved with the help of a third party, such as a pastor or counselor. Whenever possible, such methods should be pursued and exhausted first. Keeping things out of court is less stressful, less painful, and less expensive. A primary benefit of settling things apart from the legal system is that it avoids inflicting further trauma on the children.

In seeking visitation or custody, grandparents should attempt to communicate as cooperative a spirit as possible and always keep the children out of negotiations or conflicts. However, the children's wishes should be considered when they are old enough to voice an opinion.

GRANDPARENTS AND THE LEGAL SYSTEM

After all other options have been exhausted, however, sometimes grandparents must go to court if they are ever to see their grandchildren. Every state now allows grandparents to petition the court for visitation rights. Increasingly, grandparent visitation is being thought of as the *child's* right, as well.

Visitation laws vary from state to state. Some states require a good reason for a petition for visitation to come before the court (parental divorce or death are recognized as good reasons). Other states have no prerequisites. Still others consider whatever is in "the best interests of the child" to be paramount. No matter where you live, if you decide to pursue the legal right to visitation with your grandchild, it is vital that you secure competent legal counsel. Your local bar association can refer you to someone with experience in third-party visitation issues.

The decision to seek custody or visitation rights can be the beginning of a frustrating journey into unknown territory. Before you meet with your attorney, you may want to do some reading. You can obtain a copy of your state's grandparent visitation law from your nearest law library. You may also want to write to some of the organizations listed at the end of this chapter. Many of them can put you in touch with other grandparents in your area whose goals are similar to yours and who are actively involved in grandparents'-children's rights issues. Often these grandparents meet together locally to support one another and to discuss their problems. Many network across their states to push for better legislation.

Grandparents seeking visitation rights should be prepared to address these issues:

- You may have to demonstrate that an ongoing relationship with you is in "the best interests of the child." For example, if the custodial parent is opposed to your visits, how would the child be affected by the tension and animosity between the adults? Would the visits interfere with the parent-child relationship?
- You may need to produce evidence showing that a positive, significant relationship existed between you and your grandchildren prior to the divorce. That is, are you seeking to continue an already established level of involvement with your grandchildren, or are you trying to create something new? The issue is the degree of emotional closeness that already exists between the grandparents and the child.
- You may have to address practical matters such as the age of the child (is he or she too young for visits?) and the distance between your home and the child's home. If the distance is great, can you bear the expense of air travel, for example?

GRANDPARENT CUSTODY

A *Washington Monthly* article stated, "When French grandparents were polled a few years ago about what they wished to devote their retirement to, the answer most frequently given was 'to help the children.' They mean it. One third of infants are looked after by grandparents while their parents work; one half of children spend their annual holidays with their grandparents."[2]

As a culture, Americans have come to regard grandparenting a bit differently than the French. Needless to say, many American grandparents aspire to goals other than caring for their grandchildren during their retirement years. Today, grandparents in the U.S. are extremely diverse. The stereotypical and romanticized image of the doting, cookie-baking, all-wise grandparent has been more or less replaced by one that is more "symbolic." Symbolic grandparents, according to a University of Wisconsin study, "tend to be younger and more involved with jobs or community activities" and "take active pleasure in their grandchildren but don't spend as much time with them."[3] If you are more "symbolic" in your grandparenting style, chances are you never planned on—or even entertained the thought of—raising your own grandchildren. Yet, as a grandparent in the 90s, you may find yourself doing exactly that.

If you are facing the prospects of raising your grandchildren, you are by no means alone. Today 4 percent of all Caucasian children and 12 percent of all African-American children reside with their grandparents. That amounts to 3.3 million children who live with Grandma and Grandpa instead of with Mom and Dad—an increase of more than 40 percent over the

2. Katherine Boo, "Grow up twenty-somethings. You *can* go home again," *The Washington Monthly*, April 1992, 35.
3. Carolyn Jabs, "Generations," *Sesame Street Magazine Parents' Guide*, November 1988, 22.

past decade. No figures are available regarding other ethnic groups living in the U.S. The spiraling rate of divorce is partially to blame, along with the three other "Ds"—death, desertion, and drug abuse.

Grandparents often seek custody of their grandchildren when the children are being neglected, abused, or the parents are addicted to drugs or alcohol. They wind up with the job of raising a second family because they want to remove their grandchildren from desperate circumstances. Many grandparents who tackle the job of parenting the second time around—in their 50s, 60s, or 70s—discover that it is tougher than when they did so the first time. "We just don't have the stamina," said one grandmother. "I'm so tired at night that my eyelashes hurt."[4]

In addition to the "energy crunch," parenting in later life tends to have an impact on social life. While other couples are finally beginning to enjoy the freedoms that come with an empty nest, those raising grandchildren seem to reside in another world—one that revolves around carpooling, soccer games, Cub Scouts, trips to the pediatrician, and Happy Meals at McDonald's. There is a financial pinch as well. Raising children on a retirement income is a challenge. Some grandparents with custody receive child support, but the average amount is usually far less than most foster parents receive. Consequently, second-time-around parents must often forego opportunities they had looked forward to doing during their retirement years, like redecorating the house, cruising the Caribbean, or wandering the country in a Winnebago.

---

4. Joanmarie Kalter, "It's Gran and Poppa—Instead of Mommy and Daddy," *New Choices*, July/August 1993, 28.

Why do these grandparents reorder their priorities, stretch their budgets, and lay aside some of their dreams? The answer is simple: love. Most of those who take on the challenge of raising their own grandchildren do not regret their decision to do so. They would rather become surrogate parents than see their grandchildren wind up in foster care or continue living in an emotionally or physically abusive environment.

THE EXCEPTION TO THE RULE

As described in previous chapters, children of divorce who recover best often have adults other than their parents who care deeply about them and who stay involved in their lives. Grandparents who fill this role can be extremely positive life-long influences on kids after their parents divorce. That's why, as a rule, I strongly encourage grandparents to pursue this kind of involvement with their grandchildren. But there is an exception to the rule.

Grandparents who have serious personal problems such as alcoholism or another addiction, or a history of verbally, physically, or sexually abusing family members—especially their children or grandchildren—*should not* seek close involvement with their grandchildren. Instead, these grandparents should detach from their children and grandchildren and seek professional help immediately.

Here's why. Divorce is often "hereditary." That is, the family patterns that typically lead to divorce are passed from generation to generation. If, for example, a grandparent abused his or her own sons and daughters in any way, when they grow up and have children of their own, it is highly likely they will pass the abuse on to *their* children. These grandchildren, in turn, will grow up to pass the abuse on to the next generation. Cycles of abuse and addiction will not go away without deliberately addressing the problem with the help of a professional.

If you know that you played a part in the chain of family abuse or addiction, you can take the lead in stopping the cycle. *Instead of pursuing visitation or custody, detach now and get help.* It will be difficult to admit what has happened—perhaps the most difficult thing you have ever done in your life. But admitting the truth to yourself, to God, and to a caring, trained professional, is the first step toward healing the wounds of your family. It is the single most important action you will ever take for yourself, your children, your grandchildren—and for the future generations of your family.

Remember that God is always on the side of truth. He promised that knowing the truth would set us free (see John 8:32). Psalm 51:6 says, "Behold, You desire truth in the inward parts." Jesus even said, "I *am* . . . the truth" (John 14:6, emphasis mine). As you move courageously in the direction of healing and growth, remember that honesty and humility are your allies, and that God is your closest, most constant companion.

PART IV

A New Beginning

13

Holidays, Birthdays, and Family Traditions

The best part about my parents' separation is that now I get *two* birthday parties and *two* Christmases!

—*a ten-year-old boy*

CHANGE IS INEVITABLE

Divorce always brings change, but holidays, birthdays, and family traditions can showcase the changes of divorce in bold relief. The degree of change will depend upon the closeness of your family, both emotionally and geographically. At the very least, there will probably be one or more persons missing from family gatherings like birthday parties. In many cases, there will eventually be new folks present—new spouses, step-grand-children, new friends and extended family.

Every change in family celebrations or traditions is laden with potential for fresh grief. Holidays can illumine the losses of divorce as nothing else can. But most of the emotions associated with holidays and divorce can never be anticipated. They come in the form of surprises. How do you know what you will feel when you open a box of Christmas ornaments and see one your former son-in-law made for you by hand? How can you anticipate the feeling of receiving a Valentine from a grandchild you love but may never see again? What will it be like to celebrate your birthday without your daughter-in-law's traditional gift of a beautifully decorated homemade cake? In every family, at every holiday, the losses of divorce can be particularly amplified.

These thoughts need not sadden you but rather, prepare you. Divorce is a series of gradual adjustments. As the years go by, family holidays and birthday celebrations will affirm the family identity but also serve as milestones of change.

TIME TO HEAL

The first months following separation are likely to be the most difficult. Since holidays and family occasions are interspersed throughout the calendar year, chances are good that a special day of some sort will come up during this tender and painful period. Often the goal of family members is simply to make it through the holiday; enjoyment doesn't factor in. In fact, until all the "firsts" have been experienced—the first Christmas, the first Easter, the first children's birthday party— the entire family is navigating uncharted waters.

Once a special occasion has occurred and family members know experientially that they can live through it, facing the second year is a little easier. By the third year, holidays and family get-togethers are far less painful, and family members may even start to look forward to them again.

Your adult child, newly separated or divorced, will struggle with holidays because the expectations, stresses, and financial concerns that accompany most people's holidays are greatly compounded for those facing family disruption. The thought of attending a Thanksgiving dinner without your spouse or decorating the house for Christmas all by yourself intensifies feelings of abandonment and loneliness. Be prepared for the fact that your child will probably have a rough time.

Facing holidays and special occasions as a single person, rather than as a married person, is a big adjustment. It takes time to get reoriented, and it takes walking through those special days a few times to build the realization that, "Hey, I can do this!" As a parent, you face an adjustment too. Someone will be missing from the usual place at your table. Because of that, there may be a noticeable damper on holiday festivities for a year or two. But there are no shortcuts to healing these wounds; time is the only cure.

MAKING CHANGES

It is inevitable that holidays and other celebratory occasions will be changed in some way by divorce. Sometimes it is the silence that speaks most loudly to a broken relationship. Marie lamented, "Father's Day and birthdays we never get one thing from our son. It doesn't matter on my part, but it hurts me for his dad. They were so close."

Changing family traditions is not always necessarily a bad thing, however. To the extent that the old traditions highlight the fact that someone is missing, change can actually be preferable. Part of the acceptance of divorce may involve moving on to new traditions and family interactions. The sooner new traditions are initiated, the sooner everyone can take another step toward healing and moving on in a new lifestyle. Being consistent and traditional is fine, but it's also a good idea to begin some new special events that will grow into traditions of their own.

As a grandparent, you can even suggest some special new traditions. For example, you might take your son or daughter and/or grandchildren to see "The Nutcracker" each year at Christmas, if this is something they have never done before. Maybe they could attend church with you on Christmas Eve or spend the night at your house on Halloween. What will be feasible in your own family, of course, depends on factors such as how far away your relatives live, the ages of your grandchildren, your finances, and your physical health. With some creativity, you can probably help your son or daughter institute some new traditions that will help them make the transition from celebrating as a married person to celebrating as a single.

For you, one tradition which may grow out of the divorce is the practice of celebrating a "holiday after the holiday" with your grandchildren. Since children often spend their holidays alternately with each parent, you may not get as much time—or any time—with them on some holidays. One of the enjoyable ramifications of divorce for a child is sometimes getting to celebrate two or more Christmases and two or more birthdays. If your time to celebrate comes before or after the actual day, so what? Make the most of it and you may find that the "birthday after the birthday" is just as much fun and maybe even more relaxed for everyone.

How to Help

Given the painful time your family is going through, what is the best way to handle the holidays? What can you do to help your son or daughter? Here are a few practical tips.

1. *Encourage your son or daughter to only do those things they truly have energy and money to do.* Give them "permission" not to send out cards, or bake cookies, or decorate, or buy gifts they cannot afford. Your child is in a crisis emotionally, if not financially, so go out of your way to assure them that they need not conform or perform according to certain expectations. If necessary, you can explain to family and friends that things may be a bit different this year, but it's necessary to make some changes at this time.

2. *Make yourself available to pick up some of the slack left by the missing spouse.* Putting the presents under the Christmas tree alone on Christmas Eve is a bittersweet experience. If you live nearby, your son or daughter might appreciate company during moments such as this. Some experiences are just more special when shared, especially with a family member. Visiting Santa at the mall, shopping for and wrapping gifts, giving kids' birthday parties, addressing Valentines to take to school—these are examples of some times when your companionship may be an encouragement to your child.

3. *Make sure your son or daughter will not be alone on a holiday.* This is especially important if he or she will not have the children. Make plans with your child well in advance of the holiday so that they will have something to look forward to. Invite your child to be with you, or plan to visit, or at least encourage her to make plans with friends or other relatives. The first time an ex-spouse comes to pick up the children on Christmas is almost unbearably painful. Try to be sure your child is not left for a somber, tearful evening alone.

4. *Refocus on the true meaning of the holidays, and help your son or daughter to do the same.* Reflecting on the value of family and friends and on the care and presence of God is a great comfort.

Difficult times are typically a period of soul searching and reevaluating priorities. As painful as holidays are just now, they can also be opportunities for personal growth and family bonding.

ATTITUDE

Helping your family through the holidays really starts with the right attitude. A balanced outlook is the best approach. If you expect (or try to force) a joyous time of celebration and family unity, you set yourself and others up for disappointment. But if you go into the holiday expecting that things will be horrible, you actually contribute to the problem by projecting a negative attitude.

A proper balance includes a realistic understanding of the difficulties your family may encounter and anticipation of the good things that will surely be a part of the upcoming event. Lowering your expectations a bit will enable you to be understanding and tender with your child and grandchildren, yet upbeat and festive as well.

A nineteenth century psychologist, writer, and educator named William James said, "The greatest discovery of my generation is that a human being can alter his life by altering his attitudes of mind." His words still ring true. Often it is the attitude about our circumstances, rather than the circumstances themselves, that needs changing most. You probably do not like what divorce has done and will yet do to the traditions and celebrations of the family. But there is no way to undo what has been done. You can only move forward.

Resolve to be open, flexible, and creative when it comes to holidays and family traditions, and you will be making the very best of your circumstances.

14

Remarried . . . With Children

Divorce almost always leads to remarriage.

—*Eda LeShan*

Y ou may not be ready for the idea just now, but as parents of a divorced child, you need to consider the possibility that your son or daughter will remarry. Perhaps he or she is even talking about it already. "How can we go through this again?" many parents wonder. So many issues still remain unresolved. Your child put all his love and support into the last relationship (as you, the parents, may have also) and look what happened. How can this adult child go into another marriage without extreme caution and ambivalence? How can you find the emotional energy as a parent and onlooker yet also involved?

The thought of a potential remarriage raises conflicting emotions. On one hand, the parent wants the child to be happy, and the parent feels much less responsible for the child's well-being if they have a spouse. But consider all the things that could go wrong: How will the new spouse fit into the family? How will the family "blend" if there are children? How will the grandparents get along with these new children . . . the step-grandchildren? There is good reason for concern!

One father said, "I have these strong feelings about marrying and remarrying, but I didn't see any reason why my daughter should grow old by herself. Yet, I was concerned that whoever she met—and I knew she was going to, she's human—would put her through the same thing again."

The parents may, in fact, still be grieving the loss of their ex-in-law. How can you now embrace a new in-law? Unless it's been several years, it is normal for parents to feel a loyalty conflict and to have misgivings about how readily this new partner can be embraced.

Second marriages have a higher divorce rate than first time marriages (about 60 percent). Contrary to popular belief, people don't learn from their mistakes but tend to repeat them in new relationships. (One helpful resource is *Love Gone Wrong*; see the Recommended Reading.) If you are concerned for your adult child, speak your mind at least once, clearly, but then let him live with his own decision. Remember that showing support and encouragement is not the same as giving approval. If your adult child believes that she is in love, then there is probably little you can do to change her mind. Networking with other friends who still have influence in her life will sometimes help, but other than lots of prayer, there is little more you can do when marriage is imminent.

Spiritual Ground Rules

In today's society, most people don't think twice about the rights and wrongs of remarriage after divorce. Supposedly if you struck out once, or even twice, you still deserve another time at bat. This may be your own assumption.

There are many Christians (and some of other religious persuasions) who believe that remarriage is wrong. They believe that the Bible teaches that divorce doesn't count in God's eyes and that a person is still morally bound to a spouse so long as he or she lives. Based on some of Jesus' teachings, they believe that any remarriage after a divorce is adultery.

If these are topics of concern for you, read Jay Adams's book, *Marriage, Divorce and Remarriage in the Bible.* This resource may help resolve the questions about your son or daughter's right to remarry.

The Bible makes it clear that God hates divorce. God wants married people to stay married in warm, loving relationships. The Fresh Start Seminars do not encourage people to divorce but urge reconciliation wherever possible. However, human beings are sinful. We make mistakes. We hurt each other with the mistakes we make. In a perfect world, there would be no divorce. But this world is not perfect. Much of Scripture includes God's guidelines for making the best of a bad situation. God even set forth legal guidelines for divorce: Obviously He didn't favor it, but if it were done, He wanted to make sure it was done fairly. The Bible consistently urges special care for the victims of bad situations—the poor, the powerless, the widows, the orphans.

Within that context, it is proper to treat most divorced people (of both sexes) as *widows*. Their previous relationship has died. Their attempts to resuscitate it have failed. Just as a widow is free to remarry after a spouse's death, it is legitimate for a victim of divorce to remarry—*if* that divorce was based on biblical grounds, and after the proper attempts to breathe new life into the old marriage have failed.

This is not the situation in which someone says, "Oh, I'm tired of this spouse. I want to try another." That is still adultery, plain and simple, and it leaves many victims in its wake. Nor is this the situation in which a couple says, "The old spark just isn't there anymore." Marriage isn't based on sparks but on commitment. These are not biblical grounds for divorce, and the marriage vows need to be kept.

But once a biblical divorce has occurred, the parties need to repent for the part played in the breakup, pick up the pieces, and move on. Scripture speaks of God's mercies being "new every morning" (Lam. 3:23). If the old has truly died, new life can be enjoyed. There are women whose husbands (and men whose wives) walked out on them eight, ten, twenty years ago. They have faithfully waited for their spouses to come back, even after the spouses remarried. They believe that they are still morally bound to the one they first married. Such faithfulness and persistence to reconcile is laudable, but in reality when the marriage finally dies, Scripture allows them to pick up, move on, and create a new life, perhaps with another husband.

From a Scriptural perspective, the major issue is not remarriage but rather whether or not the divorce was biblical. In simple terms, the biblical grounds for divorce are (1) sexual immorality and/or adultery on the part of the spouse or (2) abandonment by an unbelieving spouse. Christians are to offer forgiveness in both of these situations, but if a spouse is unrepentant, a divorce is legitimate. Generally speaking, with a biblical divorce there is the right to remarry.

What if the divorce was not biblically based? Perhaps it occurred before your child became a Christian, or he divorced for all the wrong reasons. Perhaps she is even the one who *had* the affair—how does God view that adult child?

Two basic principles apply:

1. The person should do whatever possible to redeem the situation. Ask forgiveness. Seek reconciliation. Make amends.
2. If the ex-spouse has remarried or refuses all attempts at reconciliation, accept God's forgiveness and enjoy newness of life.

No matter the situation, take the time and effort to study the Scriptures and to consult with your own church leaders if there are any concerns about the legitimacy of your child's possible remarriage. Obviously the decision to remarry is not yours to make; it is your child's. But it is important for you the parent to honor God's Word, agonize through the issue one more time, but then act in grace when it comes to this complex issue.

THE RIGHT TO REMARRY

Just because the adult child has the right to remarry, doesn't mean that it's right for every adult child to remarry. People remarry for many reasons, but some of them are not very smart. Some of these reasons include:

- I need financial security
- God meant for me to be married

- Too much sexual pressure
- I'm so lonely
- I'm too busy to date around
- I need to settle down and start eating better
- My children need a father

All of these statements reflect very real problems, but marriage is not the solution. If any of these issues seem like the primary reason that your son or daughter wants to remarry, proceed with extreme caution. As a parent there is very little that you can do to change an adult child's mind, but you may be able to raise enough questions to help her stop and think about her decision.

When grandchildren are involved, there is another layer of issues to consider. Trying to blend a family is a very difficult task, which few couples have managed successfully. Some people even postpone the wedding for many years even though they are very much in love, just because they wanted to wait until the children were out of the house.

OVERCOMING THE EMOTIONAL BAGGAGE

As the parent of a divorced child and hopefully a more neutral observer of the relationship, you may be aware of some of the baggage that is being overlooked if your child is considering remarriage. Encourage her (and the fiancé) to consider these issues and perhaps recommend a good premarital counselor. This is an excellent idea for all marrying couples; but for those who have been married before, special attention needs to be given to unresolved conflicts from the previous marriage.

A parent must also be willing to recognize that some of the baggage may be from your child's upbringing—in other words, from you! A parent probably recognizes the baggage in the fiancé's family: "They don't know how to show their feelings" or "They don't know the proper ways to celebrate Christmas." But it is easy to be unaware of your own contribution to the child's baggage. It is important not to contribute to any problems the marrying child may be facing: A meddling parent is not welcome when it comes to weddings. A lot will depend on the existing parent-child relationship. If a good "heart-to-heart" can take place, that may be the best help of all. However, if the relationship is strained and parental suggestions are unwelcome, then it is probably best to back off.

Not all baggage is necessarily burdensome. The values and standards taught the child, the caution instilled for making good decisions, and the commitment to make marriage a permanent relationship, is invaluable. But with divorce and remarriage unfortunately, the negative baggage usually far outweighs the positive. Even after careful assessment, prayer, and counseling, baggage can be buried so deeply that it doesn't come out until well into the new marriage.

One couple who had remarried hit a crisis after a year when the wife went shopping and came home late. She had said that she'd be home "about dinnertime," which to the husband meant five P.M.

When the wife drove up a little after six, the husband was frantic with anger and concern. "Where were you? Do you know what time it is? You could have been splattered in the streets somewhere. How was I to know where you were? Why didn't you call?"

At first the wife responded fairly calmly. "It's only six o'clock. I said I'd be home *around* dinnertime. Why are you so upset?"

When the husband continued to vent his frustration, the wife suddenly said, "Wait, I think there's someone else in the room with us."

Bewildered, the husband looked around, knowing that they were obviously alone.

"What are you talking about?" he asked.

Astutely she responded, "I think your ex-wife is in the room with us. Your reaction tells me that there's more going on here than a general misunderstanding about the time I was expected home."

The wife was right. Even though the previous marriage had ended ten years ago, the incident had brought back an unconscious memory. The former wife went out, and the husband didn't know where she was, whom she was with, nor when she would be home. As suspected, she was being unfaithful. Those painful memories were part of the baggage brought into the new marriage.

As a parent, you can take the opportunity to provide some wise counsel to your son or daughter and hope your own experiences will be brought to bear in making their attempts at a new marriage more successful.

PRACTICAL QUESTIONS

There are many practical questions raised by parents looking at a child's possible remarriage. Answers are difficult since situations and people are so varied. The level of parental involvement depends largely on the kind of relationship maintained with your son or daughter and the adult child's level of maturity. Here are a few examples.

How Involved Should the Parents Be in the Wedding?

Most second marriages are not as large or involved as first-time weddings. However, there are many variations. Assuming the son or daughter is fairly mature, he will probably want to make his own plans and arrangements. Many will pay for everything themselves, so all the parents need to do is find out what to wear and when to show up.

In other cases the adult child expects the parents to be much more involved and part of the decision making. If so, relax and enjoy the role. Ideally the parents feel privileged to be able to go through this again with the son or daughter.

What Do the Parents Say to Friends and Relatives?

People will take their cues from the parents when announcing a second wedding. If Mom and Dad are upbeat and positive about the news, others will be also. People are genuinely happy when loved ones find new love, unless someone indicates there is something wrong.

Second marriages have a greater tendency to be between people from very different backgrounds—religion, culture, social status—so expect unusual customs and varied traditions in the ceremony.

What About Gift Giving?

People will naturally give gifts to the bride and groom. There is no reason to feel guilty or apologetic about inviting guests. They want to be part of the celebration and are happy to give a gift. Most people (including you the parents) may want to consider gifts such as money, savings bonds, or airline tickets since most remarrying couples have more than enough household goods. Feel free to ask the couple of their needs, and then spread the word. People appreciate knowing they are giving something which will be needed.

What About the Children?

A remarriage is a very stressful time for any children involved. Blending a family is one of the most difficult tasks a family can take on. This is discussed in greater detail later in this chapter.

Couples with children will usually have their children participate in the wedding. This should not be forced but encouraged. In one wedding of a blended family four teenagers from the bride joined three teens from the groom in singing "We Are Family" as part of the wedding ceremony.

What About the Other Set of Parents?

Parents may be concerned about establishing a relationship with another set of in-law parents. If their son or daughter has not been divorced, the parents of the divorced child may find themselves feeling guilty or worrying about their approval. Most likely, however, they will be just as happy as you are.

There may or may not be a relationship established with them. This really depends on how well the two couples hit it off. The good news is that since the adult children are more mature, there is no need to feel forced into an artificial relationship with the other set of parents. Take the cues from them and be friendly.

What About the Family Album?

When the son or daughter remarries it's time to put away the old wedding pictures and replace them with new photos. Out of respect for the new son- or daughter-in-law, old family photos need to be put up, but not necessarily thrown away. If there are grandchildren, save the old photos for their sake. They may want to go back and reminisce about their former family and ask questions about their parents' wedding, their birth, or other family events.

WHAT ABOUT THE GRANDCHILDREN?

A remarriage will also affect the grandchildren and raises some very real concerns about how this new marriage might go. Will the new spouse be a good stepparent? How will this affect the relationship with the real parent? What will the new marriage do to visiting rights and how much will the grandparents be needed now? These questions are common to the anxiety parents feel about the adult child's new relationship.

Maintain an objective (if possible) and balanced concern for the grandchildren as the possibilities of the remarriage are explored. Objectivity is necessary because remarriage can be rationalized as "best for the children"—it makes life easier for the parents. Balance is necessary because parents' needs cannot be ignored just because remarriage may be difficult for the children (grandchildren).

The truth is, a remarriage is one more disruption for grandchildren that takes from two to five years in which to adjust. The vast majority of those who remarry say that blending their families, or just adding one new parent to the formula was *much* harder than they ever anticipated.

A remarriage is not merely a continuation of an existing family with the addition of one new member. Rather, the remarriage constitutes a new beginning—one in which every "old family" interaction is drastically changed. Adding one new person to a family of three is not one new interaction but rather six new relationships, any one of which can be sour enough to cause turmoil throughout the whole family system.

This honest appraisal is not intended to make parents even more anxious about a son or daughter's remarriage, but to warn of the difficulties ahead. Instead of thinking, "Oh good, once they're remarried, they won't need us anymore," they may need you more than ever. Parents can be a tremendous help by making themselves available as a listening ear, a constant source of encouragement and prayer, or a weekend baby-sitter so the newlyweds can get away from time to time.

Helping Your Grandchildren Cope

The following guidelines (along with the Recommended Reading) can help the parents help the adult child thinking about remarriage.

If the Former Son- or Daughter-in-Law Is Remarrying

One type of remarriage issue that has not yet been addressed but which does affect the parents, the adult child, and the grandchildren, is the remarriage of the former in-law. Both parents and children can be emotionally better prepared for such an event by considering the following.

1. *It is normal to have reactive feelings to the remarriage of a former in-law, even though there was the feeling you were completely over the divorce.* Many times this reaction takes the form simply of the realization that the ex-in-law is "moving on with life" and that the couple will never be reunited. This is the "final curtain." Deal with those feelings with the help of your spouse or a trusted friend. Don't let any negative emotions about the other spouse's remarriage taint your adult child or grandchildren toward the changes they will have to face. Be especially encouraging to your grandchildren since they will have to face this new family structure and accept a new stepparent. Try to stay as neutral and emotionally uninvolved as you can in front of the grandchildren, but encourage their talking honestly with you about how they view the pending changes.

2. *Encourage your grandchildren to participate in the wedding if invited.* They may resist due to perceived loyalty to the other parent and to you, but you can free them up to take part in the ceremonies. Negatively influencing them or your adult child will only hurt their relationship with *you* in the long run.

3. *Allow your grandchildren to talk about their new stepparent.* They might not be able to express their true feelings to immediate family members. You don't want to encourage their negative comments but you can at least empathize with their feelings, whether negative or positive. Once again, try to remain emotionally neutral.

4. *Unless information is especially alarming, stay out of what goes on in the other household.* Everything children say can't be taken at face value, but if it seems particularly unusual, check out the story with your former in-law at the next opportunity. For example, it's not your business if the grandchildren glee-

fully report that "Dad and Nancy had a big fight," but you may want to check out what is meant by "Dad and Nancy don't feed us when we're over there." Never jump to conclusions, but be alert, sensitive, and gracious.

5. *Even though it may be difficult, it is best for the grandchildren if you can maintain a polite relationship with the new stepparent.* There will always be occasions where it is necessary to converse with him or her, as when visiting arrangements must be coordinated. Cooperation is a must if you want to help your adult child and grandchildren through this difficult time.

The Adult Child's Remarriage

As noted earlier, your own son or daughter's remarriage may be a glorious time for the parents and immediate family, but this may prove to be a time of mourning for the grandchildren. Try to be sensitive toward them during this time and consider the following guidelines.

1. *Don't expect instant rapport between the grandchildren and the new stepparent.* These relationships take time. In fact, some don't "gel" until a year or two into the marriage. (Some never do.) If things are going great, consider the family to be blessed, but don't be surprised if the relationships become very strained.

2. *It is statistically more likely that your son or daughter will marry another divorcee, and it is also likely that this person will be someone who has very different values than those you taught to your child.* (The longer adult children are out from the parental roof the more they develop their own interests and values.) This new someone may be from another social class, a different area of the country, or a different religious background. Therefore, try particularly hard to be open-minded and supportive. Re-

member to give the person time and benefit of the doubt before passing judgment.

3. *Allow the grandchildren to talk about the new family situation.* Very likely, the grandchildren will complain bitterly about the new stepparent. Try to listen neutrally and supportively, but once again, don't take everything said at face value. Stay out of family squabbles that seem typical, and politely inquire only about any stories that seem worthy of investigation.

4. *If the new stepparent has children, these children deserve to be treated with the same respect and concern as your own grandchildren.* This new situation may take a while for you to get used to, but these relationships can be just as rewarding as the ones with your own grandchildren. Don't force relationships if you meet resistance. Work together on common projects or hobbies and wait to see what develops naturally. Watch your natural tendency to favor your own grandchildren when in front of the others, but don't bend over backwards to act as if you have known and loved them all equally either—children don't like phonies!

5. *Talk about how the holidays will be handled well in advance.* These seasonal demands on the blended family are particularly difficult. You may find there is much less time available to spend with your adult child and your grandchildren than there used to be. This is to be expected, as there is a much more complicated list of relationships to consider. You may find that a time after the holidays is much more suitable to all parties. These times can be just as special, and probably more relaxed, than those spent on the actual holiday in years past.

6. *Don't expect the grandchildren ever to love the new stepparent as much as the biological parent.* This attitude only sets up unrealistic expectations which usually end up hurting the new

parent. Encourage the grandchildren to love and express love to both of the biological parents. It is helpful if the stepparent can even have a talk with the children to reassure them that "I am not going to take the place of your real father."

7. *Allow and encourage the actual parent in the relationship to provide the primary discipline and guidance to the younger children.* As a grandparent, your proper focus is on being supportive and encouraging; let the parent raise them.

8. *Children try to play one parent against the other, and this maneuver can be used on a particularly intense level in a stepparent relationship.* Try not to get drawn into this "divide and conquer" strategy. Avoid taking sides or disagreeing with either parent or stepparent. Instead, provide a supportive atmosphere that reflects a unity of mind with all of the parents. Any disagreements can be taken up with the parents in private, but remember to "tread lightly."

9. *Keep in mind that intense feelings of anger and resentment are normal in the blended family, especially among teenagers.* Try not to personalize the anger and respond in a similar fashion. You are probably witnessing the result of years of perceived betrayal and disappointment. Be as patient and compassionate as you can be, knowing that this will be a very difficult, often lengthy transition for everyone.

15

Something Whole from Something Broken

Do not be afraid of tomorrow, God is already there.
—Anonymous

A little block of wood in an old country store displays some words that are appropriate for the aftermath of divorce. It says, "If life deals you scraps . . . make a quilt." There, painted in the middle of the words is a tiny, beautiful quilt of many colors and designs.

Many times, divorce deals out only scraps. Families are severed, traditions are altered, hearts are broken, and holiday celebrations seem as if they will never be joyous again. For a while, during the grief, all we can see are the torn and stringy bits and pieces of what used to be.

In time, though, we begin to recognize that the scraps are beautiful and valuable, too. If they are trimmed up and laid side by side, someone can "quilt" something new from something old, something whole from something torn and broken. With creativity, a pile of scraps can be crafted into a beautiful quilt—something to keep people warm and convey comfort and security, something of beauty and value that will be handed down through generations.

Divorce rips life into shreds. Being shredded is agony. Yet in this vulnerable and powerless state, as the divorced person—or the parents—endures being shredded into humble scraps, God is the Someone who can somehow make a life into something exceedingly more beautiful than originally existed. If we lay still and broken in the hands of God, He begins to tenderly quilt our lives back together. The High King of heaven produces from mere scraps something more eternally significant and of a more precious quality than we could have ever otherwise become.

HOW COULD GOD MEAN IT FOR GOOD?

When you think of the divorce of your son or daughter, and all that it will mean to your family, you may wonder how to apply the story of Joseph to the situation facing your family. How in the world could God take something as awful as divorce and "mean it for good"?

We can say that while God does not desire for divorce to occur and does not cause divorce to occur, God can take the scraps of a divorce and quilt them together to make some beautiful, ultimately good things.

The New Testament says, "And we know that all things work together for good to those who love God, to those who are called according to His purpose" (Romans 8:28). Here are some of the ways that God can, in time, work good from divorce.

Divorce Sometimes Makes Positive Changes in the Parent-Child Relationship

Patricia said, "After the divorce my parents were finally able to share feelings and opinions they had had all along about the unloving situation I was in. During the marriage I was protective and defensive and put on an air of being all right. Now my parents and I share more of an adult-adult relationship, rather than adult-child."

Polly said, "I feel closer to both of my parents and am a lot freer with my feelings and tears. We talk once a week whereas before the separation we only talked every two to three weeks. My mother has been closer to me and has expressed herself more than I ever remember."

Divorced People Often Become More Humble, More Responsible, and More Independent

Even children sense that some of the effects of divorce are positive. Looking back on the divorce of his parents, Ryan, age 16, says, "I think my Mom changed the most through all of this. She not only went to work but she started to become much more independent. You know, doing things for herself. I think I wanted to protect her from getting hurt, but in time she showed us that she was strong and that she could make it on her own."

John, whose son and stepdaughter have both gone through divorce, said, "Overall, we're pleased with where the kids are. We think that both of them have learned some tough lessons and become more mature and have some hope for the future. We're hopeful that both of them are getting stronger."

In rare cases, the understanding gained through a painful divorce can eventually help reconcile the relationship between divorced partners. Megan and her husband divorced after "He decided he wanted a divorce instead of working on our individual issues and the marriage," says Megan. In the years that followed, much personal growth occurred for both parties. "We are friends now," Megan says. "After our divorce we were able to acknowledge to each other our responsibility and part in our marital problems. We have developed a friendship over the years."

Divorce Can Stimulate Positive Growth That Can Bring Second Chances

For every member of the family, sometimes including the parents of the divorcing couple, the pain of divorce can usher in a second chance—to humbly grow, to learn from pain and failure, and to love again, with the help of God. Sometimes, due to the hard lessons of divorce, people become more capable of making a second marriage work. Though scarred by divorce, these people are happier in second marriages than they were in first marriages *because of* the growth and humility produced by their divorces.

Divorce Can Draw Us Closer to God

There is an interesting phenomenon in Fresh Start Seminars. People who attend are hungry for truth and for something to believe in. Everything they once trusted in has been shattered by divorce. As a result, they become like vacuum cleaners, "sucking up" all they can with regard to rebuilding their lives, redefining their values, and rethinking their purpose in life.

The people in marriage seminars contrast sharply with Fresh Start participants. The people who come to Fresh Start often have little money, yet they pay for the seminar, buy lots of books, study furiously, and may also attend counseling. What's the difference? Motivation! While still married, people may be remotely aware of problems in their lives, but divorce has a way of bringing problems to the forefront.

God uses whatever He can to teach us what is important in life. Painful experiences like divorce tend to burn away wood, hay, and stubble, and refocus our attention on the things that have lasting value (see First Cor. 3:11–13). All of us experience this "burning away" when we suffer disappointments, losses, and grief. And then we make our choices: Are we going to blame God and others? Or are we going to learn and grow?

Divorce is one of the most graphic ways for us to see our need to refocus and change.

Without a doubt, divorce is devastatingly painful. Yet, God can use divorce for good and for personal growth. The divorce of your son or daughter is no exception. Something good can happen in your child's life and in the life of your family, in spite of all that has taken place. One counselor has said, "This is your greatest opportunity." When the bottom drops out, you can learn to trust God; you can become more emotionally healthy; with His leading you can grow stronger and more independent.

As you look at the breakup of your child's marriage and all that it will mean to your family, dare to begin to believe that God can make something whole and good come out of something broken. As you begin to rest squarely in a trust in Him, your child will be able to draw hope and strength from you.

Recommended Reading
and Resources

Some of the books listed are available from Fresh Start Seminars, 1-800-882-2799.

Grandparenting

Jan Stoop, and Betty Southard. *The Grandmother Book: Sharing Your Special Joys and Gifts with a New Generation.* Nashville: Thomas Nelson Publishers, 1993.

Newsletters

Grandparents, Scarsdale Family Counseling Service, 405 Harwood Building, Scarsdale, NY 10583 (Write for a free copy; subscriptions are $10 a year.)

New Horizons, Grandparents Reaching Out, 141 Glensummer Road, Holbrook, NY 11741

Vital Connections, Foundation for Grandparenting, 12 Sheldon Road, Cohasset, MA 02025

Grandparent Custody and Visitation

American Association of Retired Persons (AARP) Special Projects—Midge Marvel, Anne Studner, 1200 East Carson Street, Lakewood, CA 90712

Grandparents As Parents (GAP), Sylvie de Toledo, Psychiatric Clinic for Youth, 2801 Atlantic Avenue, Long Beach, CA 90801, (310) 933-3151

Grandparents Against Immorality and Neglect (GAIN), Betty Parbs, 720 Kingstown Place, Shreveport, LA 71108

Grandparents Raising Grandchildren, Barbara Kirkland, P.O. Box 104, Colleyville, TX 76034, (817) 577-0435

Grandparents' Rights Organization (GRO), Richard S. Victor, Esq., 555 South Woodward Avenue, Suite 600, Birmingham, MI 48009, (313) 646-7191

Grandparents'–Children's Rights, Inc., Lee & Lucile Sumpter, 5728 Bayonne Avenue, Haslett, MI 48840

Grandparents in Divided Families, Marjorie Slavin, Edith S. Engle, Scarsdale Family Counseling Service, 405 Harwood Building, Scarsdale, NY 10583

Second Time Around Parents, Michele Daly, Family and Community Services of Delaware County, 100 West Front Street, Media, PA 19063, (610) 566-7540

American Self-Help Clearinghouse, St. Clare's–Riverside Medical Center, Denville, NJ 07834

Foundation for Grandparenting, Dr. Arthur and Mrs. Carol Kornhaber, 12 Sheldon Road, Cohasset, MA 02025

Helping Children of Divorce

Barr, Debbie. *Children of Divorce: Helping Kids When Their Parents Are Apart.* Grand Rapids: Zondervan Publishing House, 1992.

Sprague, Gary. *Kids Caught in the Middle Workbook for Children.* Nashville: Thomas Nelson, 1993.

Sprague, Gary. *Kids Caught in the Middle Workbook for Teens.* Nashville: Thomas Nelson, 1993.

Whiteman, Thomas. *Innocent Victims: How to Help Children Overcome the Trauma of Divorce.* Nashville: Thomas Nelson Publishers, 1991.

Divorce Recovery

Burns, Bob. *Recovery From Divorce.* Nashville: Thomas Nelson Publishers, 1993.

Burns, Bob, and Whiteman, Tom. *The Fresh Start Divorce Recovery Workbook.* Nashville: Thomas Nelson Publishers, 1992.

Fresh Start Seminars, 63 Chestnut Road, Paoli, Pennsylvania 19301, (800) 882-2799 or (610) 644-6464, FAX: (610) 644-4066

The Friends, P.O. Box 389, Fargo, ND 58107, (701) 235-7341 Hotline: (701) 235-7335 (matches people going through tough circumstances with others who have been through the same experience)

Singles Ministries Resources, P.O. Box 60430, Colorado Springs, CO 80960, (719) 579-6471 (provides a listing of ministries on divorce recovery and single parenting)

Relationships

Jones, Tom. *Sex and Love When You're Single Again*. Nashville: Thomas Nelson Publishers, 1990.

———.*The Single Again Handbook*. Nashville: Thomas Nelson Publishers, 1993.

Whiteman, Thomas A. and Petersen, Randy. *Love Gone Wrong: What To Do When You Are Attracted To The Wrong Person Over and Over*. Nashville: Thomas Nelson Publishers, 1994.

Remarriage and Blended Families

Adams, Jay. *Marriage, Divorce and Remarriage in the Bible*. Grand Rapids: Zondervan Publishing House, 1980.

Frydenger and Frydenger. *The Blended Family*. Old Tappan, NJ: Fleming Revell, 1985.

Johnson, Carolyn. *How To Blend A Family*. Grand Rapids: Zondervan Publishing House, 1989.

Wright, Norman. *Before You Remarry*. Eugene, OR: Harvest House, 1988.

Stepfamily Association of America, 215 Centennial Mall South, Suite 2127, Lincoln, NE 68508, (402) 477-7837

Stepfamily Foundation, 333 West End Avenue, New York, NY 10023, (212) 877-3244, FAX: (212) 362-7030

Single Parenting

Campbell, Ross. *How To Really Love Your Child*. Wheaton: Victor Books, 1982.

Parker, Kenneth F. and Van Jones. *Every Other Weekend.*
  Nashville: Thomas Nelson Publishers, 1993.
Whiteman, Thomas, *The Fresh Start Single Parenting Workbook.*
  Nashville: Thomas Nelson Publishers, 1992.
Single Parents Family Resources, P.O. Box 427, Ballwin, MO
  63022-0427, ATTN: Barbara Schiller (314) 230-6500
Single Parent Resource Center, 141 W. 28th St., New York,
  NY 10001, (800) 924-4109 or (212) 947-0221, FAX:
  (212) 947-0369

Counseling

American Association of Christian Counselors, P.O. Box 739,
  Forest, VA 24551, (800) 526-8673, FAX: (804) 525-4217
  (provides telephone numbers of local professionals whose
  counseling is based on Christian principles)
American Association for Marriage and Family Therapy, 1100
  17th St. N.W. 10th Floor, Washington, D.C. 20036, (202)
  452-0109, FAX: (202) 223-2329
Life Counseling Services, 63 Chestnut Road, Paoli, PA 19301,
  (610) 644-6464, FAX: (610) 644-4066 (affiliated with
  Fresh Start Seminars)
Minirth-Meier Clinic National Headquarters, 2100 North
  Collins Boulevard, Richardson, Texas 75080, (800) 229-
  3000 or (800) 545-1819, FAX: (214) 644-7056

Legal Help

American Bar Association Family Law Section, 750 North
  Lake Shore Drive, Chicago, IL 60611-4497, (312) 988-
  5584, FAX: (312) 988-5568

Christian Legal Society, 4208 Evergreen Lane Suite 222, Annandale, VA 22003, (703) 642-1070, FAX: (703) 642-1075

Mediation

Academy of Family Mediators, P.O. Box 10501, Eugene, OR 97440, (503) 345-1205 or (alternate address): 355 Tyrol West, 1500 S. Lilac Drive, Golden Valley, MN 55146, (612) 525-8670

Divorce and Family Mediators, 37 Arch Street, Greenwich, CT 06830, (203) 622-5900, FAX: (203) 622-8298

Divorce Mediation Research Project, 1720 Emerson Street, Denver, CO 80218 (publishes directory of mediation services)

Resources for Special Problems

Alcohol and Drug Abuse

Al-Anonymous/Alateen Family Group Headquarters, Inc., P.O. Box 862, Midtown Station, New York, NY 10018-0862, (800) 356-9996 or (212) 302-7240

Alcoholics Anonymous, 475 Riverside Drive, New York, NY 10115, (212) 870-3400, FAX: (212) 870-3003

National Clearinghouse for Alcohol Information, P.O. Box 1908, 5600 Fishers Lane, Rockville, MD 20850 (301) 468-2600

National Council on Alcoholism and Drug Dependents Hope Hotline (800) 622-2255

Narcotics Anonymous, P.O. Box 9999, Van Nuys, CA 91409, (818) 780-3951, FAX: (818) 785-0923

RAPHA, 12700 North Featherwood Drive Suite 250 Houston, Texas 77034 (800) 383-4673 or (800) 227-2657 FAX: (713) 929-1596

Gambling/Debt

Debtors Anonymous, (212) 642-8220 or (212) 642-8222

Gamblers Anonymous, 3255 Wilshire Boulevard Suite 610, Los Angeles, CA 90010, (213) 386-8789

Christian Financial Concepts, 601 Broad Street S.E., Gainesville, GA 30501, (404) 241-3087 (overseen by Larry Burkett, a highly regarded Christian financial counselor)

Abuse

Child Protection Program Foundation, 7441 Marvin D. Love Freeway Suite 200, Dallas, Texas, (800) 688-5437 or (214) 709-0300, FAX: (214) 709-2795

For Kids' Sake, Inc., 31678 Railroad Canyon Road, Canyon Lake, CA 92587, (909) 244-9001, FAX: (909) 244-3664

National Council on Child Abuse and Family Violence, 1155 Connecticut Avenue N.W. Suite 400, Washington, D.C. 20036, (800) 222-2000 or (202) 429-6695, FAX: (202) 467-4924

Out of Control Behavior

Tough Love International, P.O. Box 1069, Doylestown, PA 18901, (800) 333-1069 or (610) 348-7090

Overcoming Homosexuality

Harvest Ministries, 1718 Spruce Street, Philadelphia, PA 19103, (215) 985-4031

Exodus International, P.O. Box 2121, San Rafael, CA 94912, (415) 454-1017, FAX: (415) 454-7826

Intervention

Johnson, Vernon. *Intervention*. Minneapolis, MN: Johnson Institute Books, 1986.